Movie Stories:

Create your own movies

Ana Maria De la Guardia

First Edition

Hello!

We are almost ready to start the show. People are taking their seats in the theater, waiting to see what you came up with. They are getting their popcorn ready, don't leave them waiting!

Before We Begin

All good movies begin with good context. This is where places, characters, scenes, and actions are placed and given meaning, at the very start of each movie.

The middle section starts when a conflict, problem, or opportunity starts brewing. This is when our characters start to change because they want or need to; because they have to fulfill a need or accomplish a goal.

Then, there is the end. This is when the situation has been resolved either for good or for bad.

When creating a story, it is critical to always pay close attention to your characters, give them a backstory, purpose, meaning, intentions, quirks, and nuance. It is important for the characters to be proactive and forward the story instead of being reactive and just let the story happen to them.

In movies, characters have arcs. They start a certain way and make a transformation as the plot happens. There are also set-ups and pay-offs, which means that anything included at the beginning of the story should have some sort of tie-in with the story at some point.

How Movies are Made

1. Concept and idea generation.
2. Budgeting.
3. Idea development.
4. Screenwriting and scriptwriting.
5. Hiring, recruiting cast and crew.
6. Scouting locations & production design.
7. Storyboards and shortlists.
8. Production schedules.
9. Execution.
10. Shooting.
11. Editing.
12. Color, Sound and Visual Corrections and Effects.
13. Final Product.

You will be doing several of these steps in this book, so prepare yourself!

Best Practices for a Movie Story:

- Avoid too much exposition; it is better to show than to tell.
- Try to keep and maintain a central theme in your story. If your story is about love, do not make it about war. It can be about both, but there is always one main theme.
- Say as much as you can, with as little information as possible.
- The actions performed in your movie story should trigger consequences.
- There should be supporting characters and antagonists in your stories wherever is needed.
- The most important characters must solve problems and work hard to progress and achieve their goals.

Instructions

Follow the instructions of each prompt and answer on each blank space following what you have learned about storytelling. You can bounce ideas with several people or by yourself.

To make your scenes and stories better, search online for following keywords:

Scene composition, Mise-en-scène, how to make storyboards, Foley sounds.

Book Terms

There are some instructions in the book that use terms that I will explain here:

Movie Story – A detailed description of the plot of the movie. Like a short story of the movie.

Plot – Summarized version of a movie story. It includes the basics of what happens in the movie.

Trailer – A description of how the movie would play out in a trailer. Including the description of the scenes appearing on-screen or the typical narrations of old trailers from the 80s.

Storyboards – Sequential drawings of scenes including the actions in them and the dialog.

Actors – The people that will perform in your movie.

Locations - The places where the movie will be shot.

Character Development

Now we are going to learn how to develop a character. To do so, you need to bring it to life by answering the following questions:

Life

Who are the character's parents? Where does he/she live? How has his/her life been? Try to create a story of what happened to him/her. How was his childhood and early years like?

Personality

What type of person is the character? What quirks does the character have? In what way does the character portray himself or herself? What type of temperament does the character have?

Customs

What are his/her hobbies? What does he/she like to do?

Attire and Physique

What does the character look like? How do he/she dress or do his/her hair? What is the character's fashion sense?

When writing a story, it is good to know who your character is so that he or she can participate in your story in a more realistic and believable way.

A mad scientist creates a fast-spreading disease, the good guy is a superhero vigilante. Who is this superhero? Can you write the full story of the movie? What is the theme of the movie you are creating? Give your movie a title. What locations would you chose?

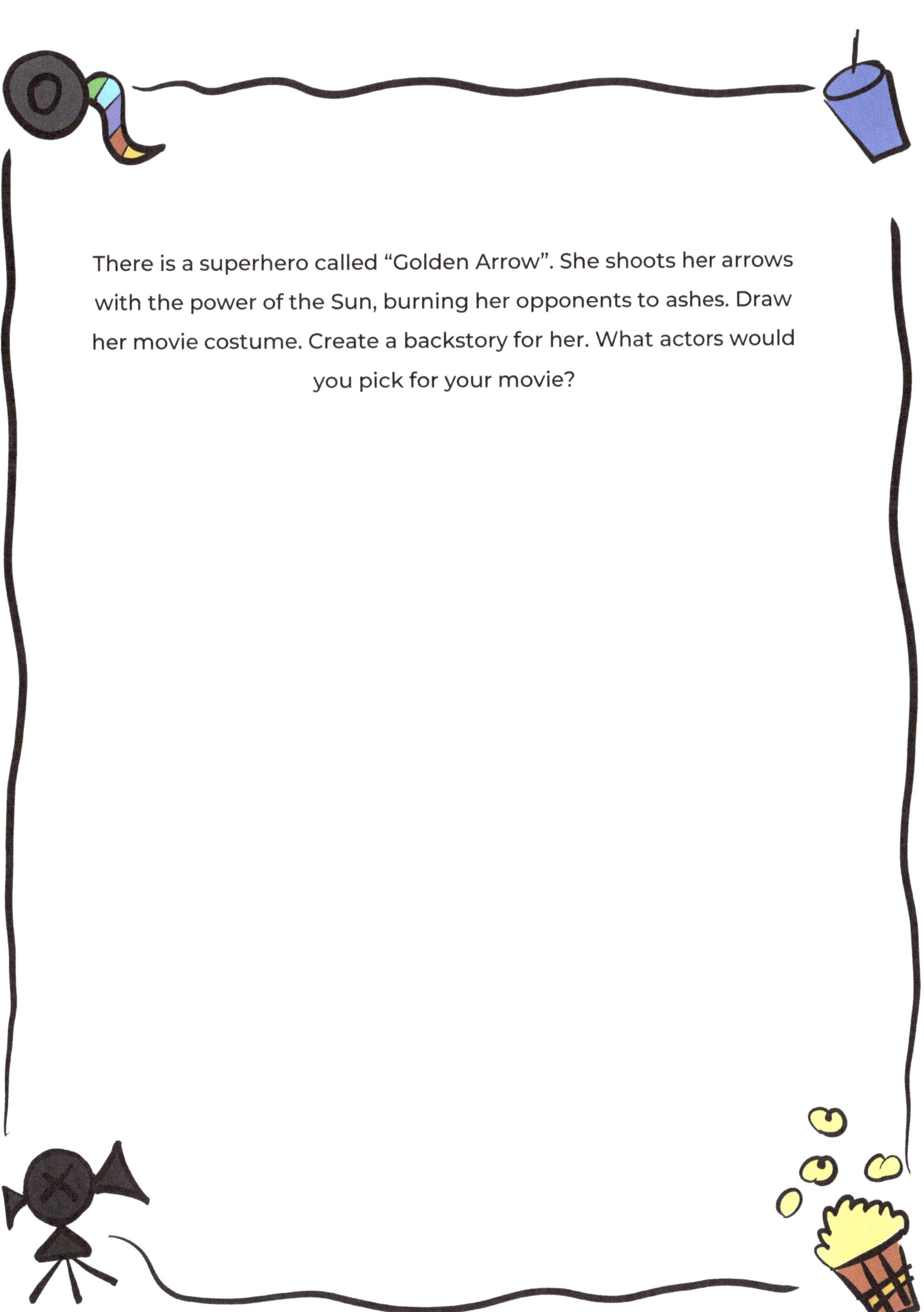

There is a superhero called "Golden Arrow". She shoots her arrows with the power of the Sun, burning her opponents to ashes. Draw her movie costume. Create a backstory for her. What actors would you pick for your movie?

There is an evil villain called Spider who confuses his opponents with a web of lies while stealing all the money, exploding cities, and creating chaos. Create the costume.

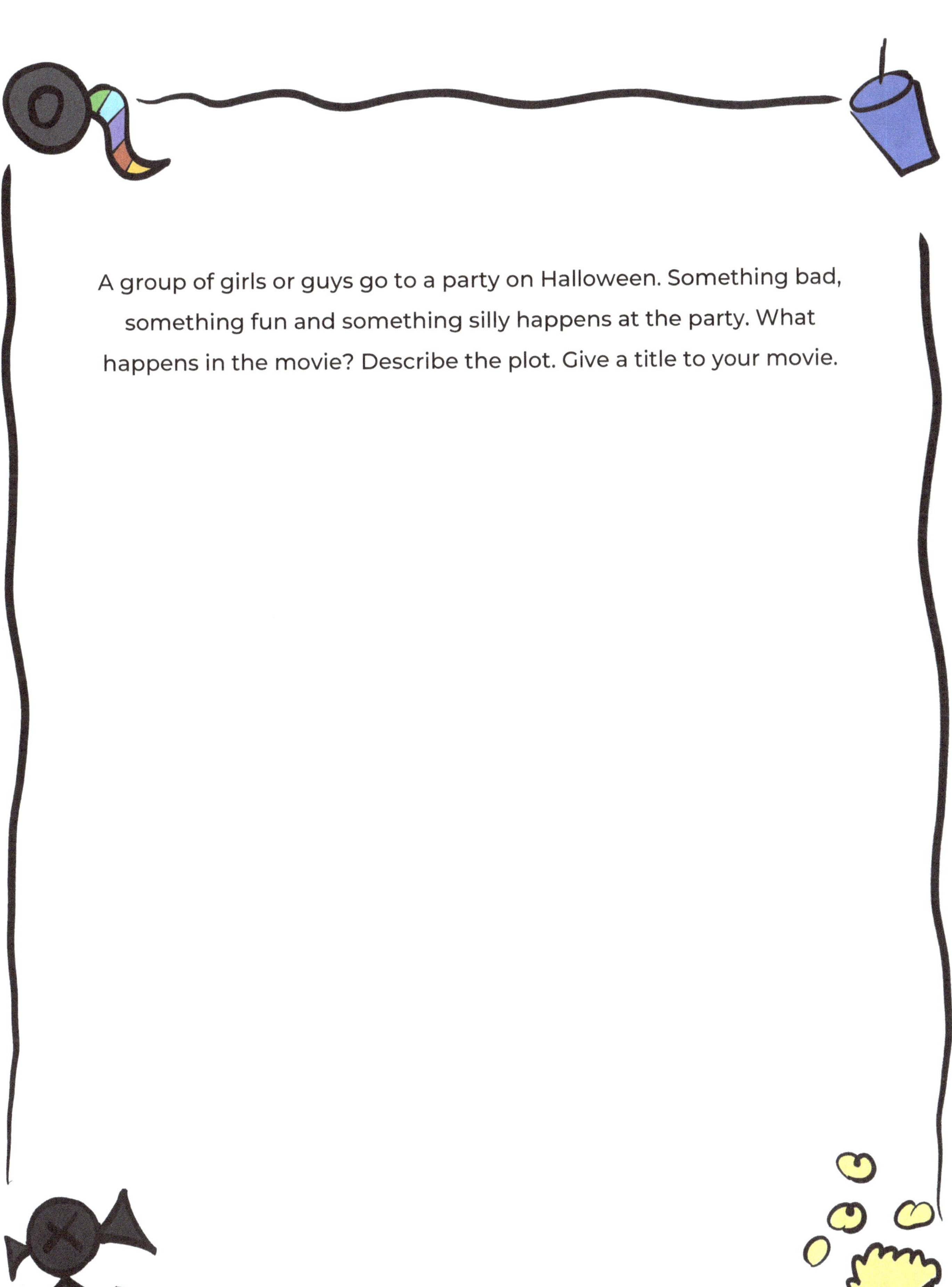

A group of girls or guys go to a party on Halloween. Something bad, something fun and something silly happens at the party. What happens in the movie? Describe the plot. Give a title to your movie.

–"It's a dog-eat-dog world" is the message of the movie. Can you create a movie based on this quote? Write it down and give your movie a title.

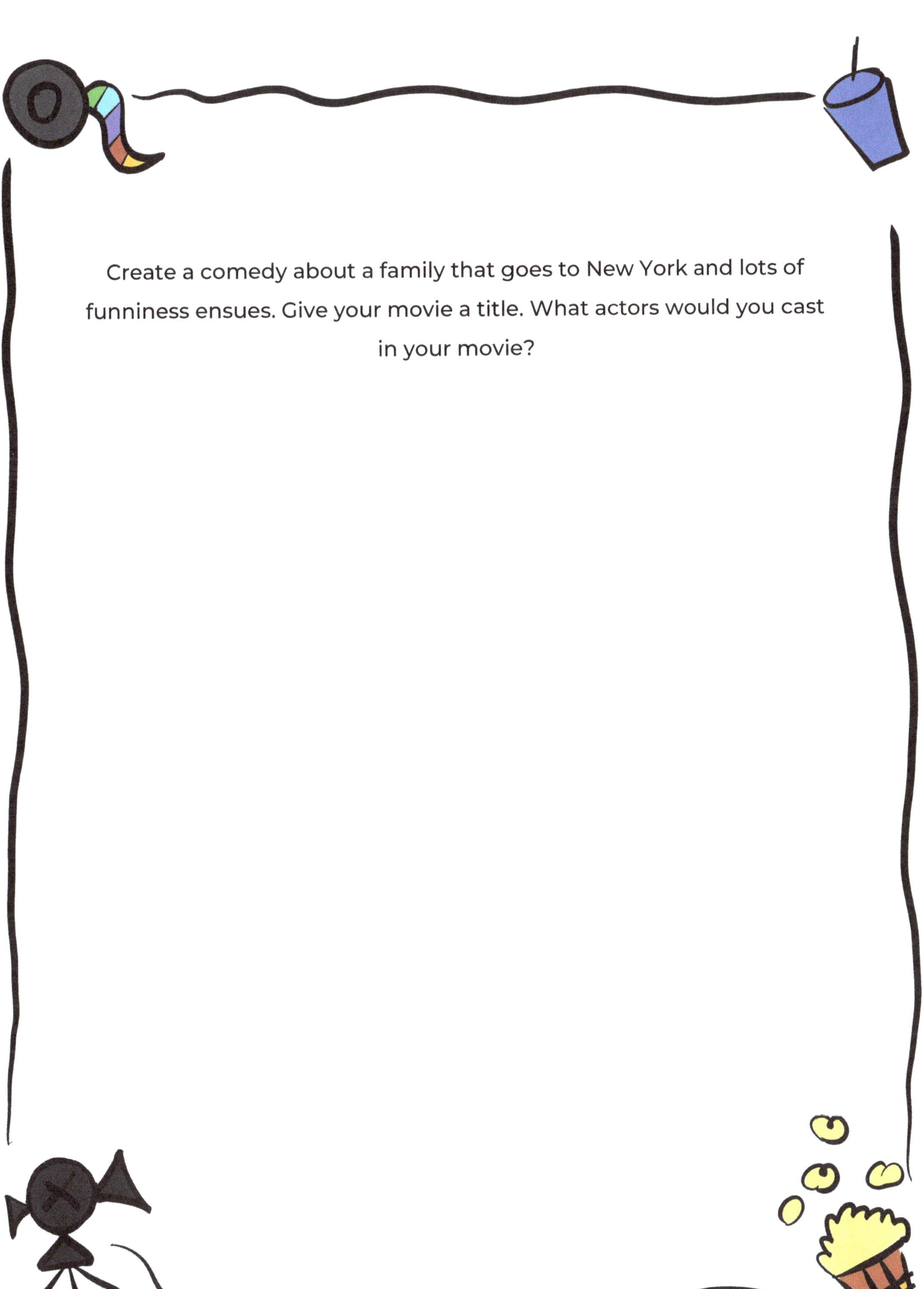

Create a comedy about a family that goes to New York and lots of funniness ensues. Give your movie a title. What actors would you cast in your movie?

– "I will never forget you," said one character. Write the dialog of this scene. Provide a title for the movie, based on this scene.

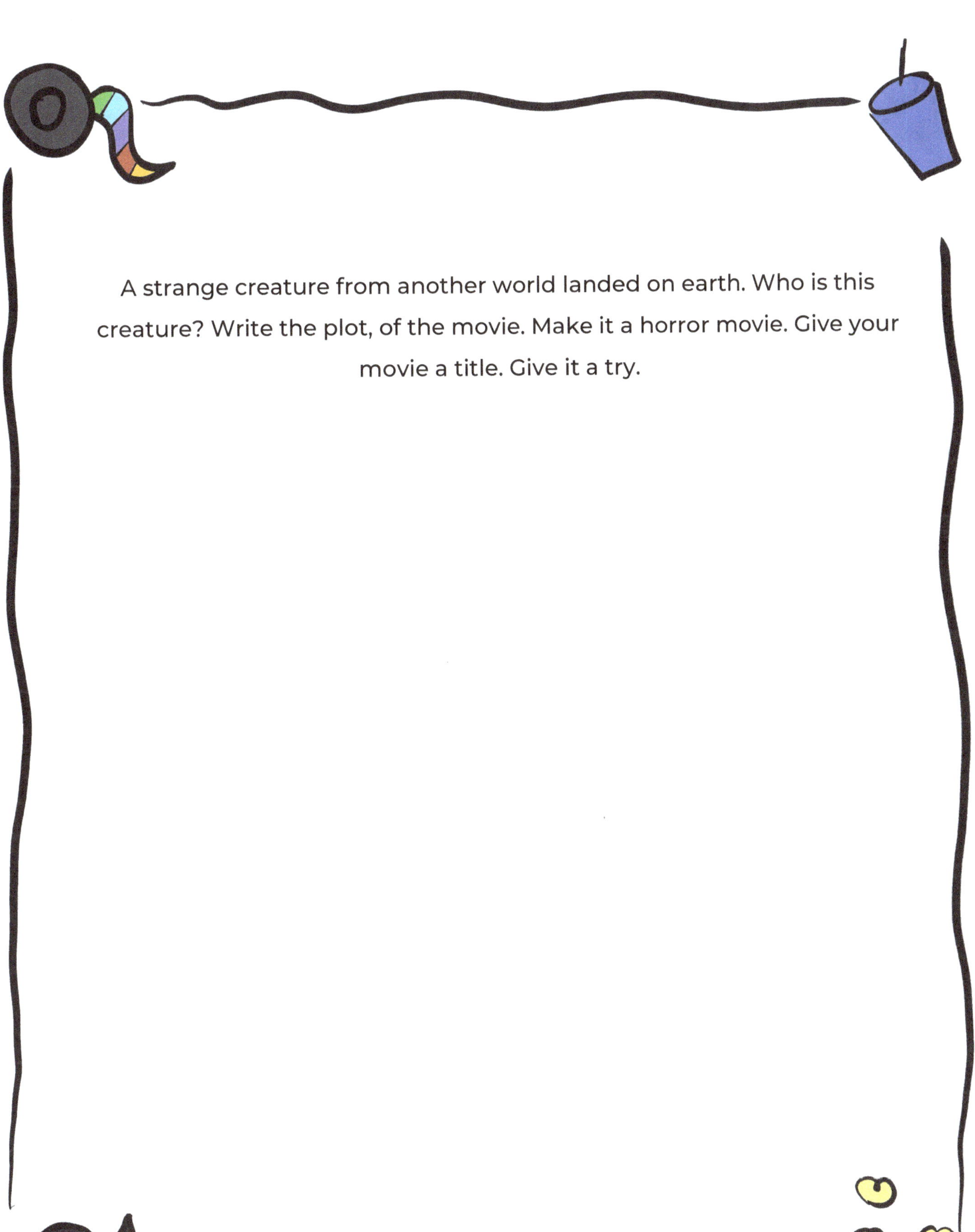

A strange creature from another world landed on earth. Who is this creature? Write the plot, of the movie. Make it a horror movie. Give your movie a title. Give it a try.

Create a different story about a creature that landed on earth but make it an action flick. Provide a title for your movie. Who would you cast?

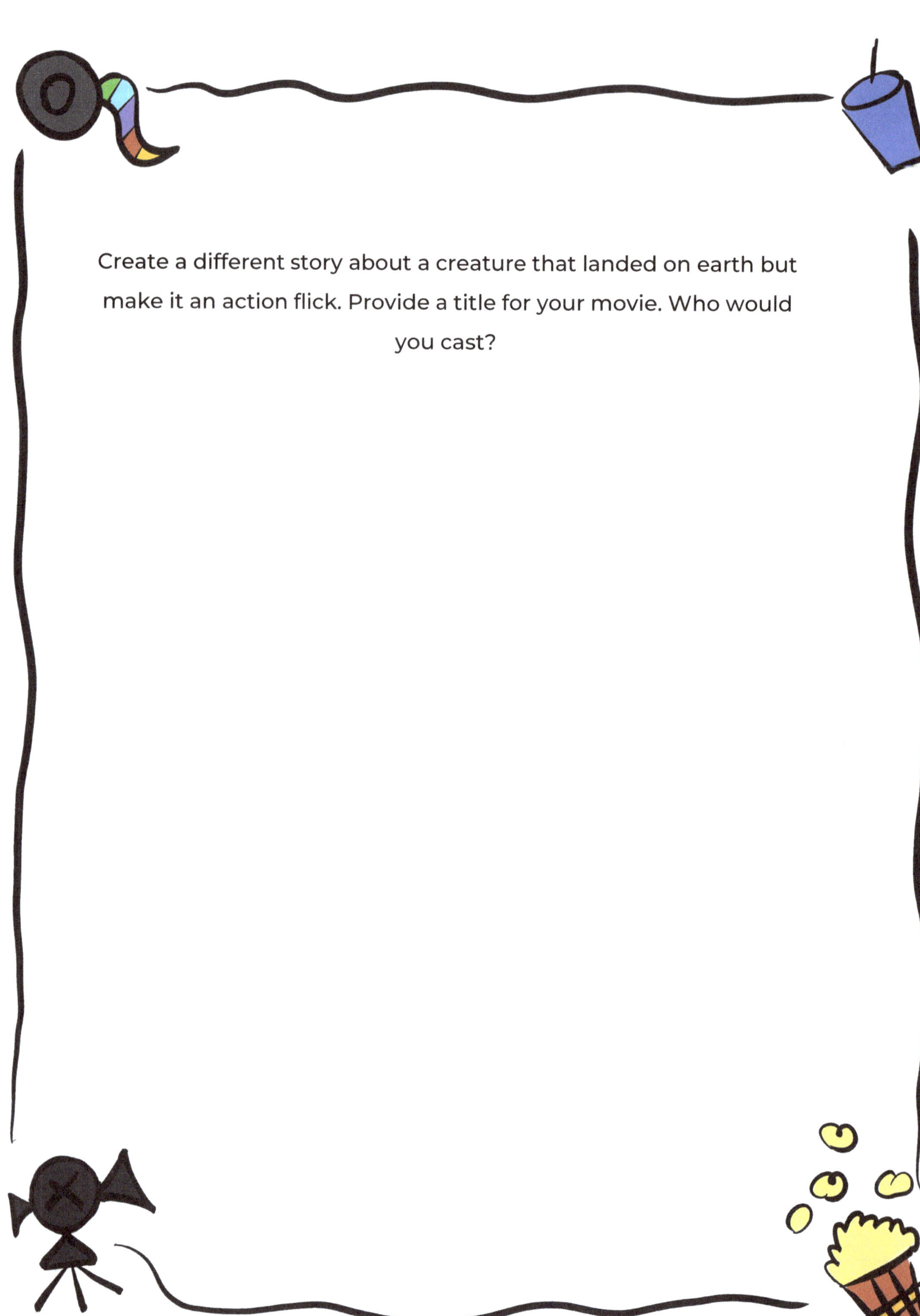

Write in less than 5 sentences, the plot of a silly romantic comedy about two neighbors who hate each other. Give your movie a title. What locations would you chose?

First, write the name of three characters in a piece of paper, three locations and three items. Then set a timer for 1 minute 30 seconds. In that time, write a love story featuring these three characters, the locations, and the items.

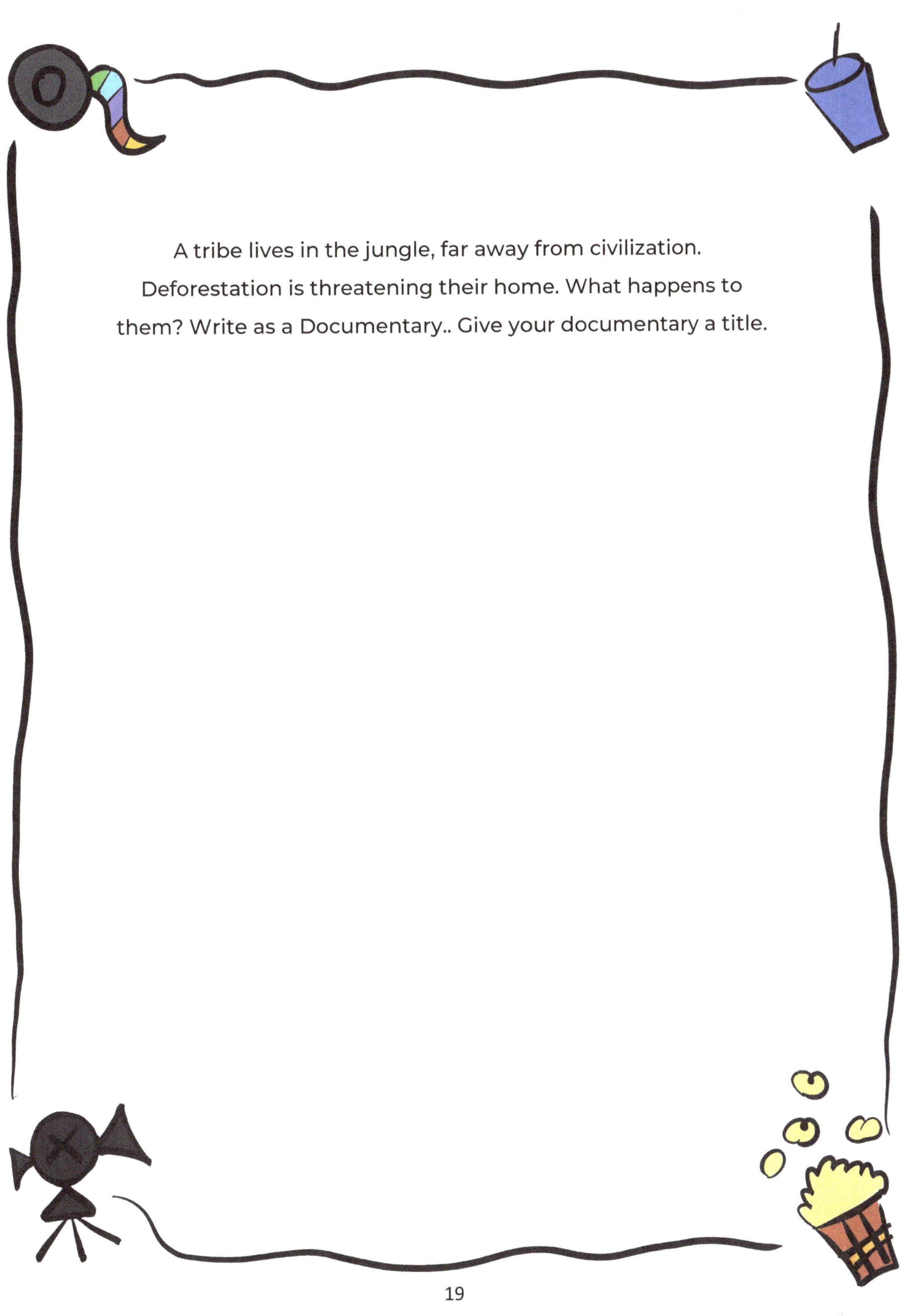

A tribe lives in the jungle, far away from civilization. Deforestation is threatening their home. What happens to them? Write as a Documentary.. Give your documentary a title.

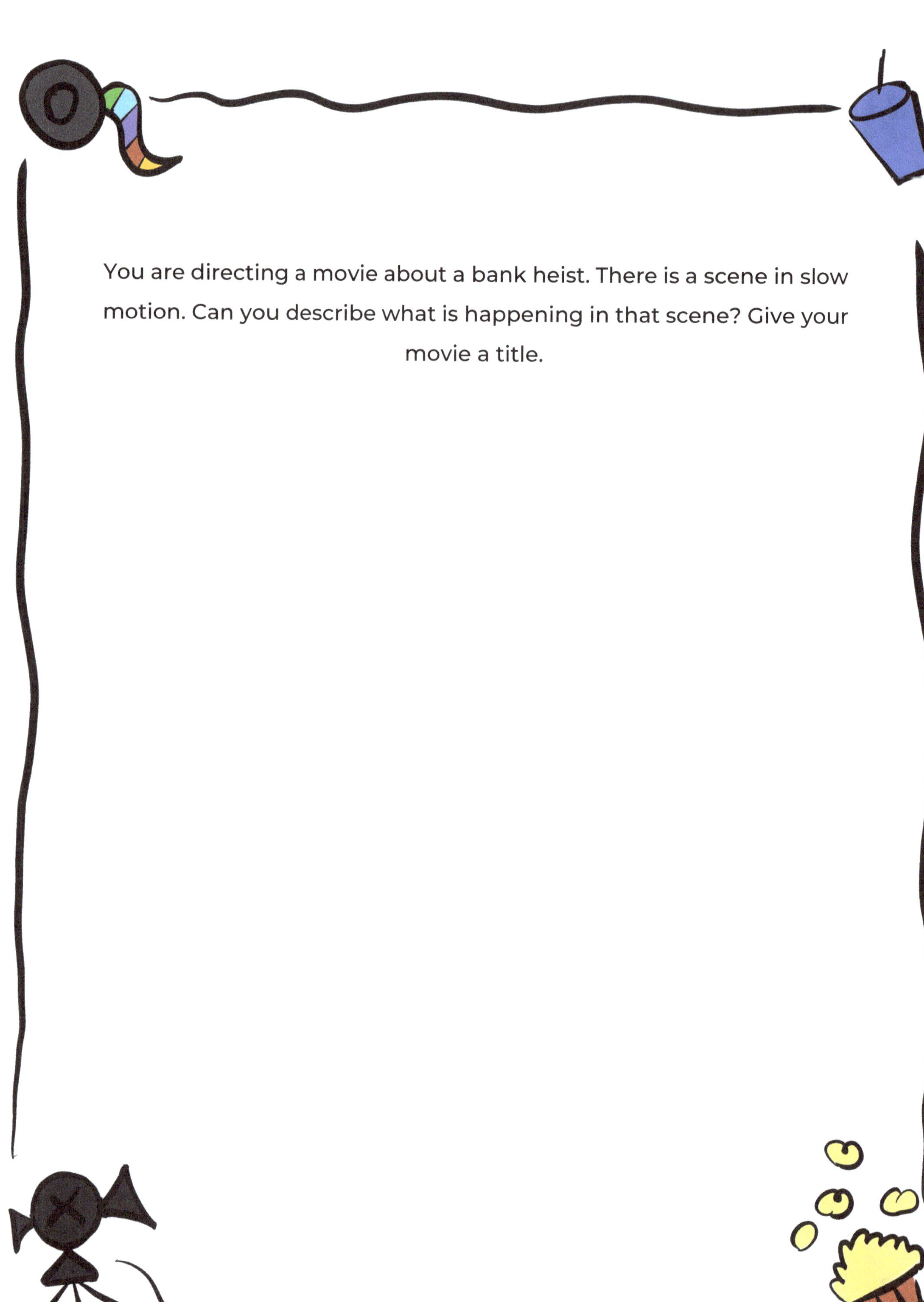

You are directing a movie about a bank heist. There is a scene in slow motion. Can you describe what is happening in that scene? Give your movie a title.

You are directing a movie about a silent killer. Can you explain who the silent killer is and how he kills? What else happens in the movie? Write it down. Give your movie a title. Who would you cast?

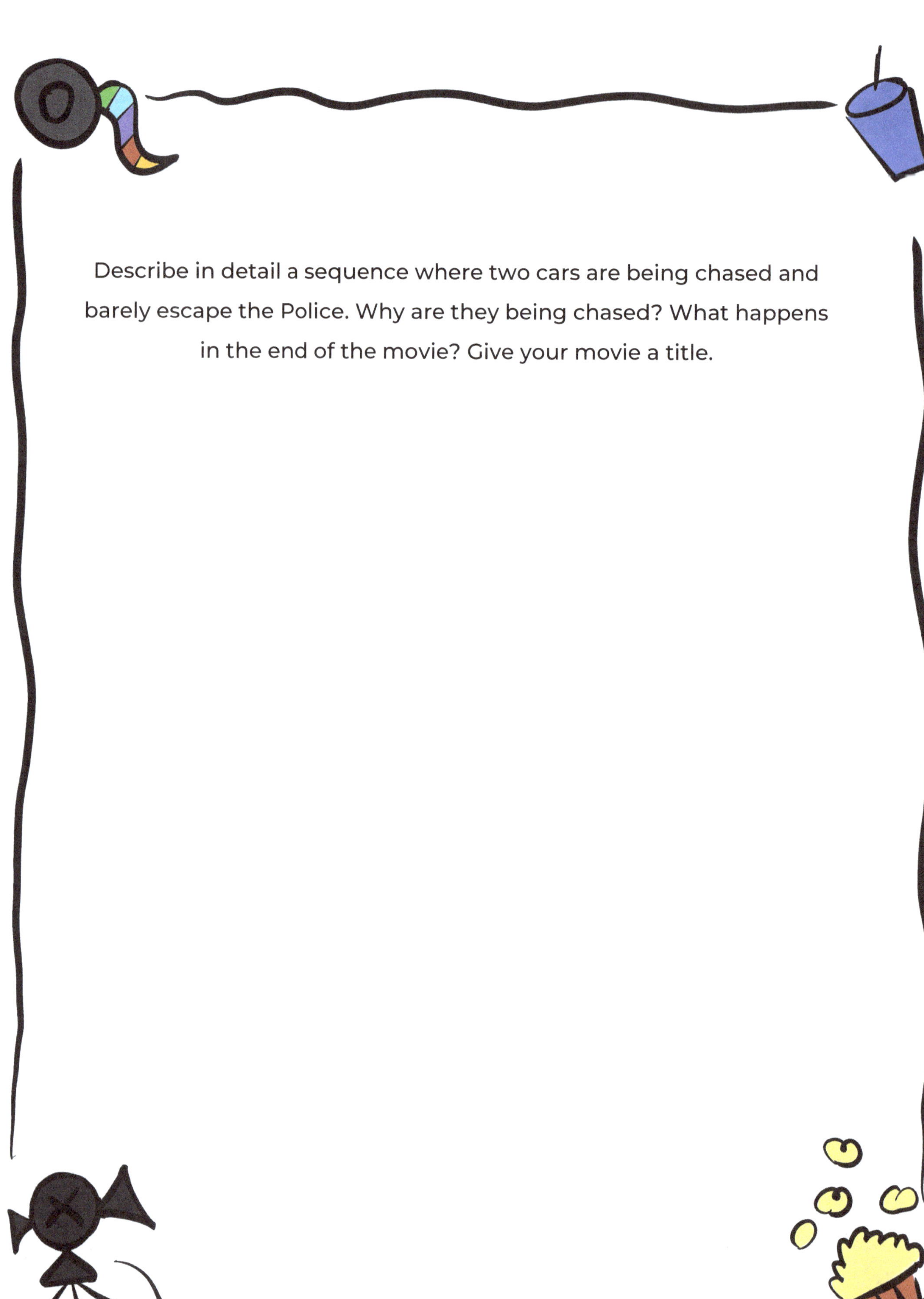

Describe in detail a sequence where two cars are being chased and barely escape the Police. Why are they being chased? What happens in the end of the movie? Give your movie a title.

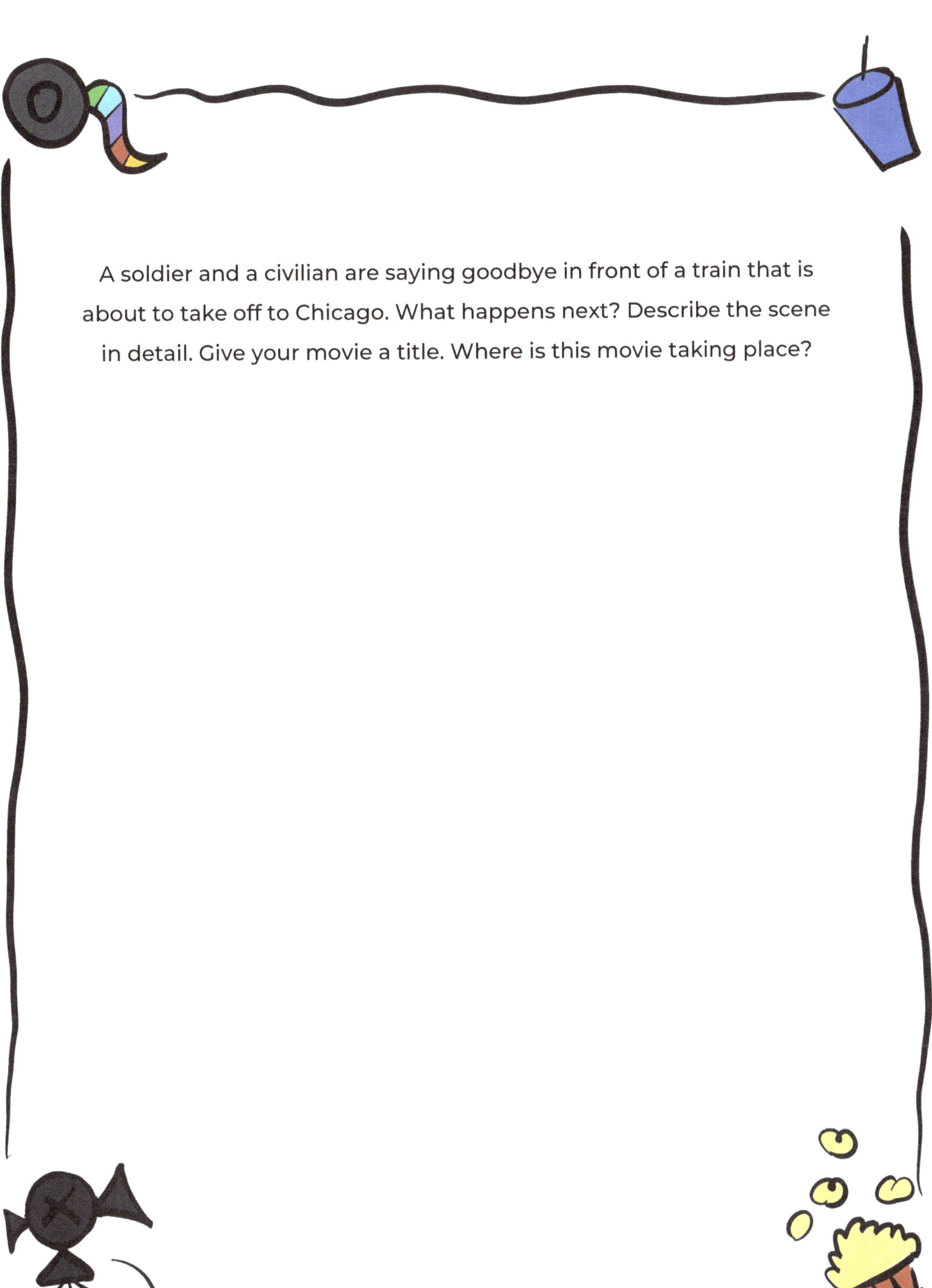

A soldier and a civilian are saying goodbye in front of a train that is about to take off to Chicago. What happens next? Describe the scene in detail. Give your movie a title. Where is this movie taking place?

An evil mastermind promises not to explode a bridge filled with cars if the good guys do something. What will it be? Describe in detail. Give your movie a title. Describe the context of the movie.

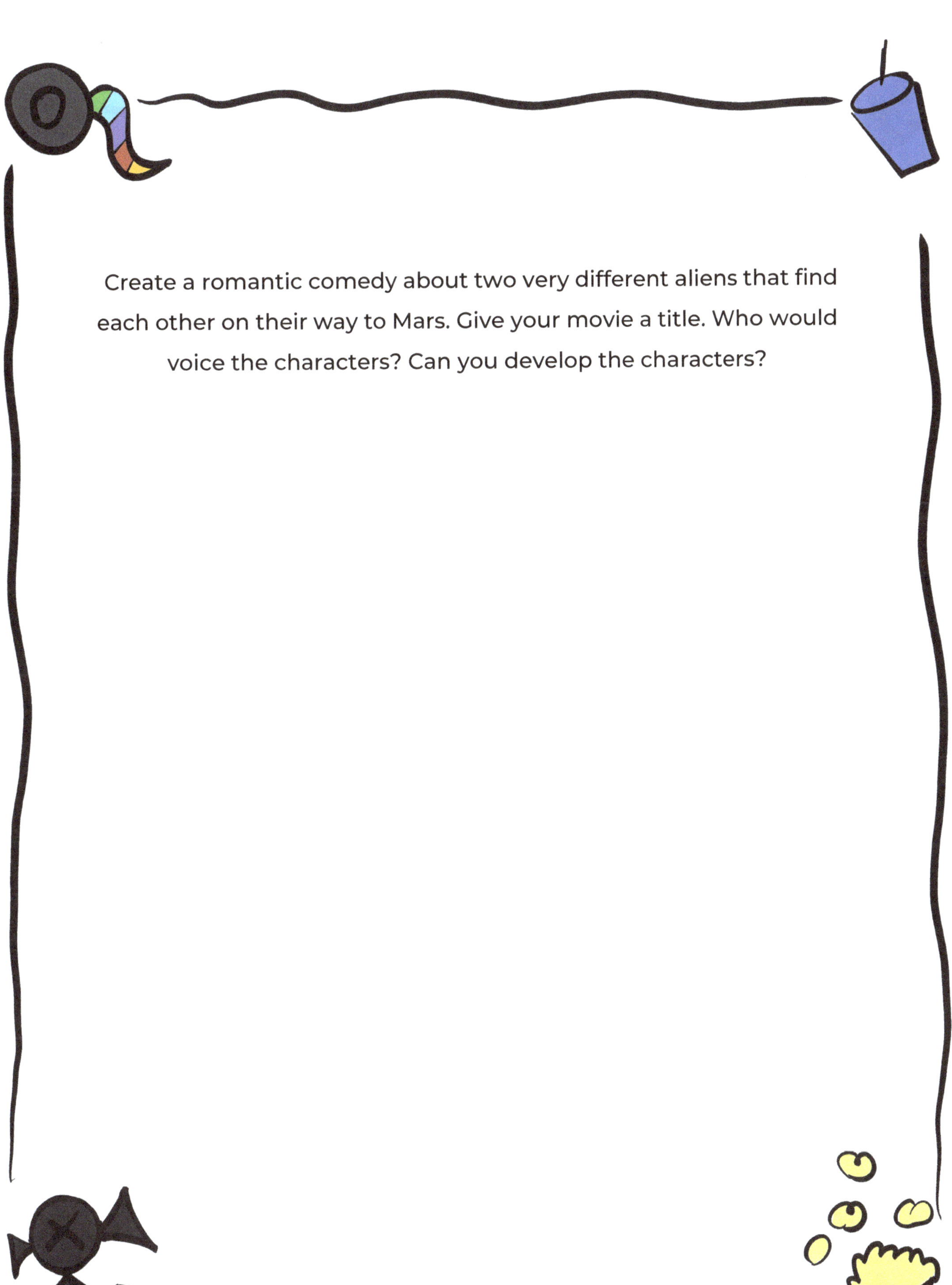

Create a romantic comedy about two very different aliens that find each other on their way to Mars. Give your movie a title. Who would voice the characters? Can you develop the characters?

Create a sci-fi movie about a strange mythical power only a boy has. The boy lives on the streets of a futuristic Manhattan. Give your movie a title. Develop the character.

Two giant Gorillas are fighting to the death over a female Gorilla in the middle of a city. While fighting, they are destroying buildings and causing chaos, until the female Gorilla stops them with her mind. What happens next? Write the trailer of the movie. Give your movie a title.

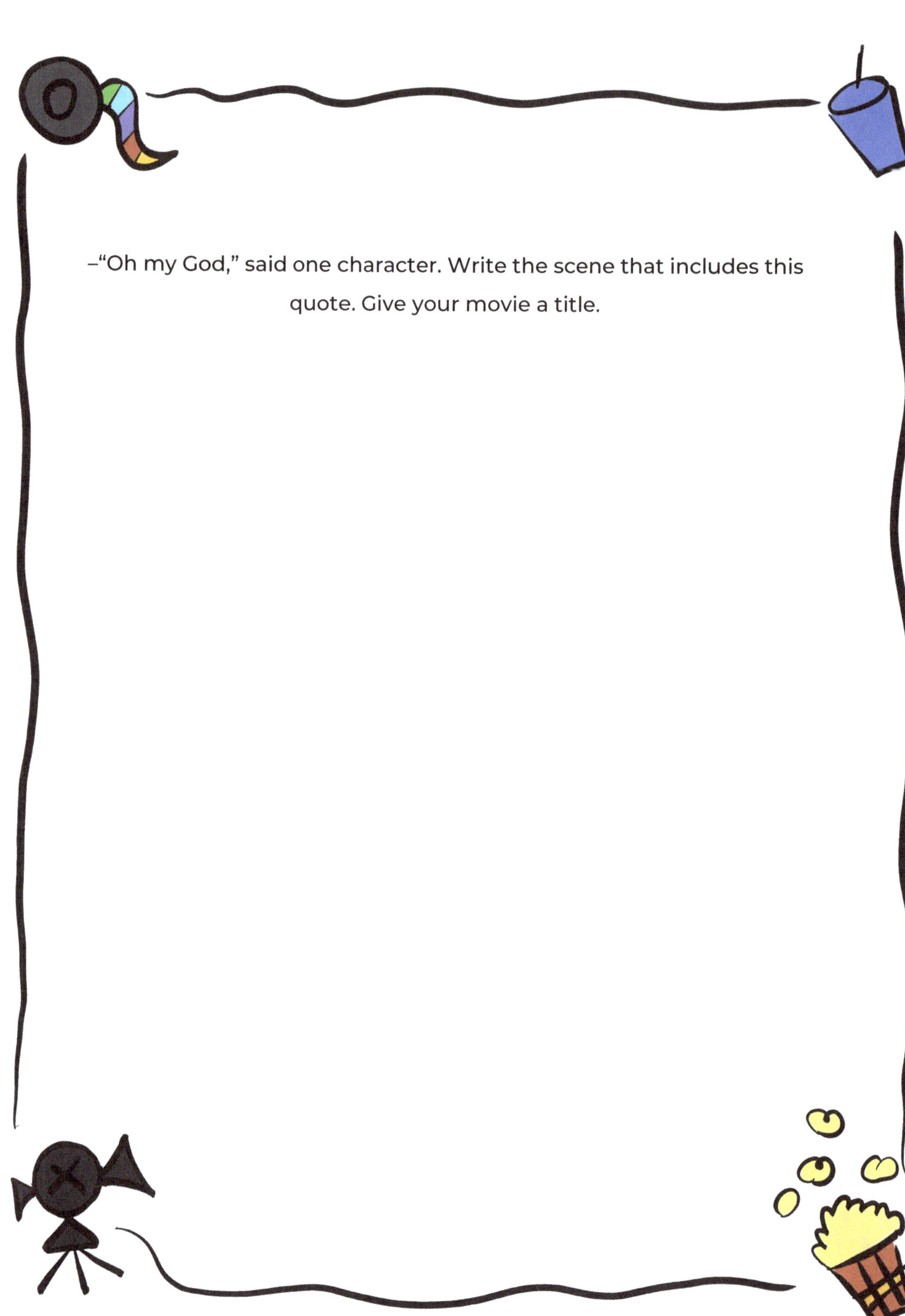

–"Oh my God," said one character. Write the scene that includes this quote. Give your movie a title.

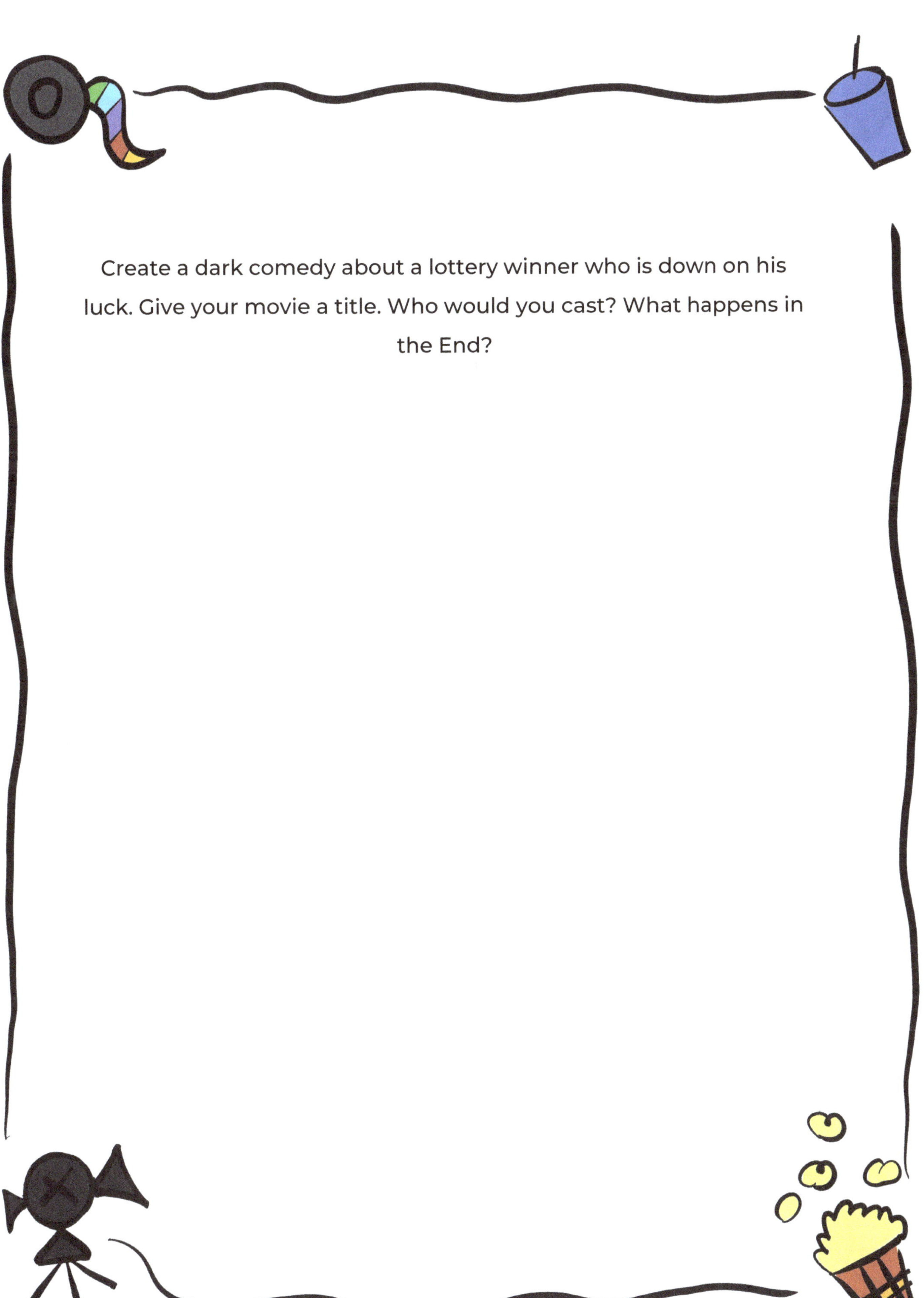

Create a dark comedy about a lottery winner who is down on his luck. Give your movie a title. Who would you cast? What happens in the End?

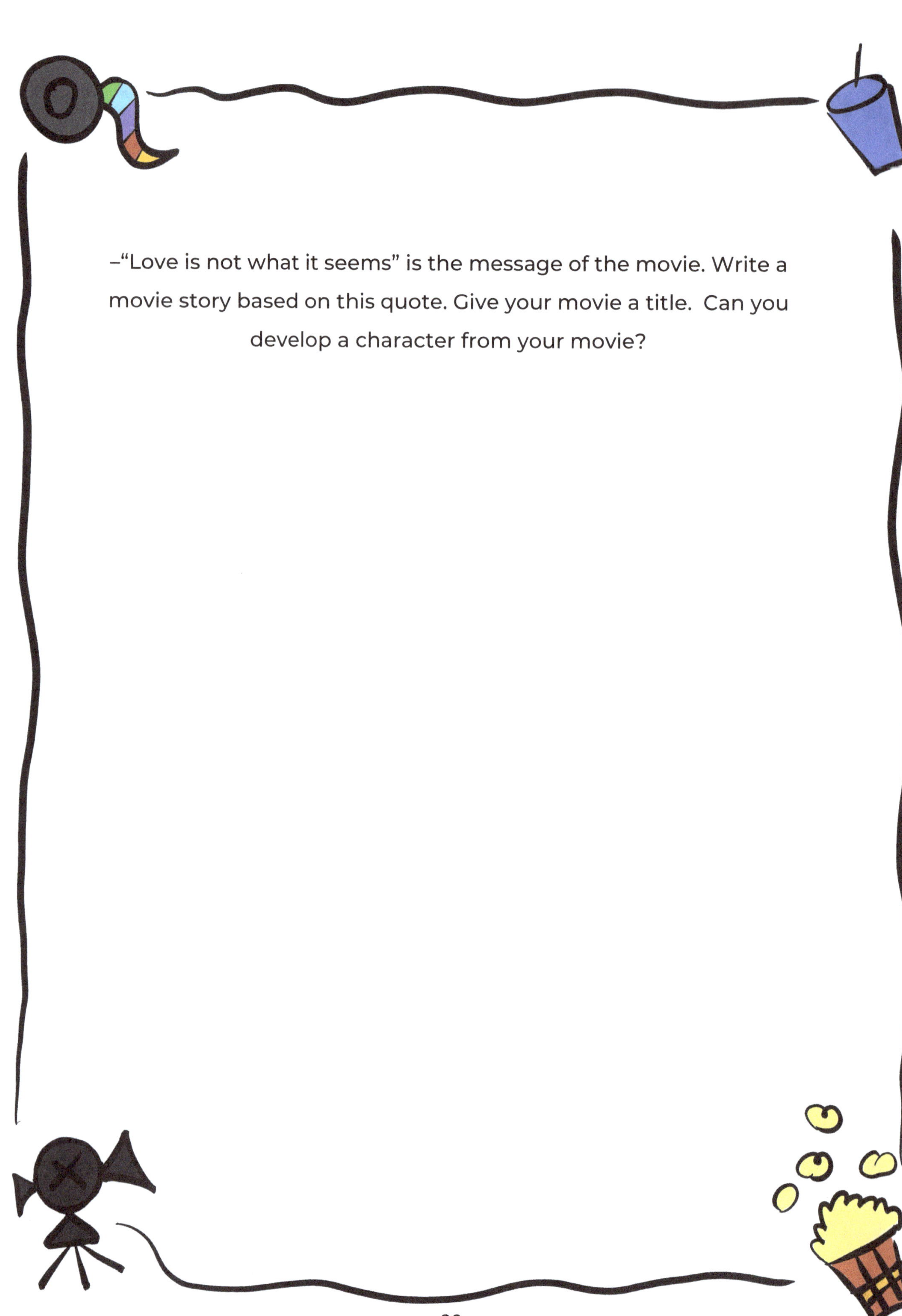

–"Love is not what it seems" is the message of the movie. Write a movie story based on this quote. Give your movie a title. Can you develop a character from your movie?

A group of superheroes are trying to save the world from killer robots. Who are the superheroes? Describe what happens in the movie and create original superheroes. Give your movie a title.

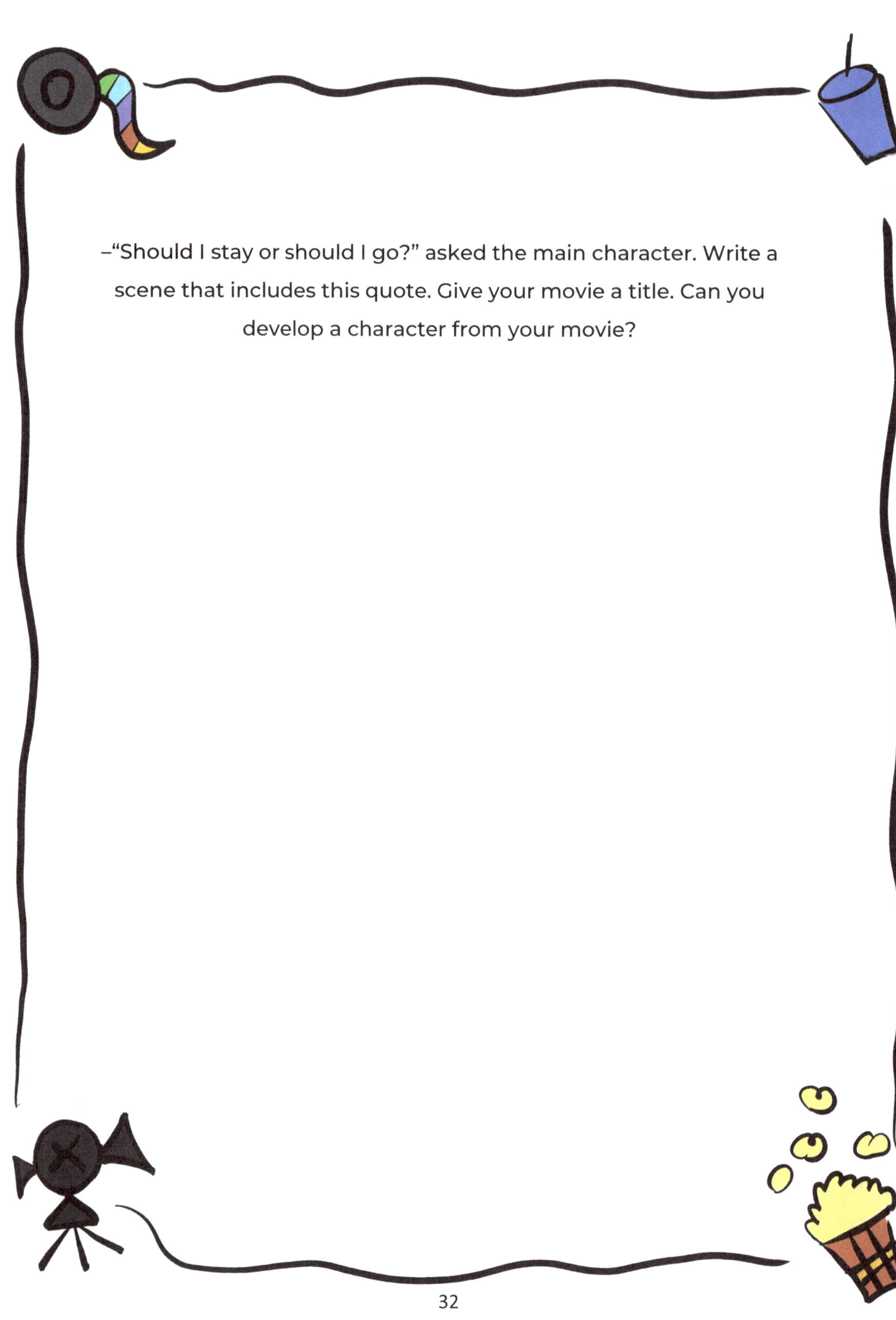

–"Should I stay or should I go?" asked the main character. Write a scene that includes this quote. Give your movie a title. Can you develop a character from your movie?

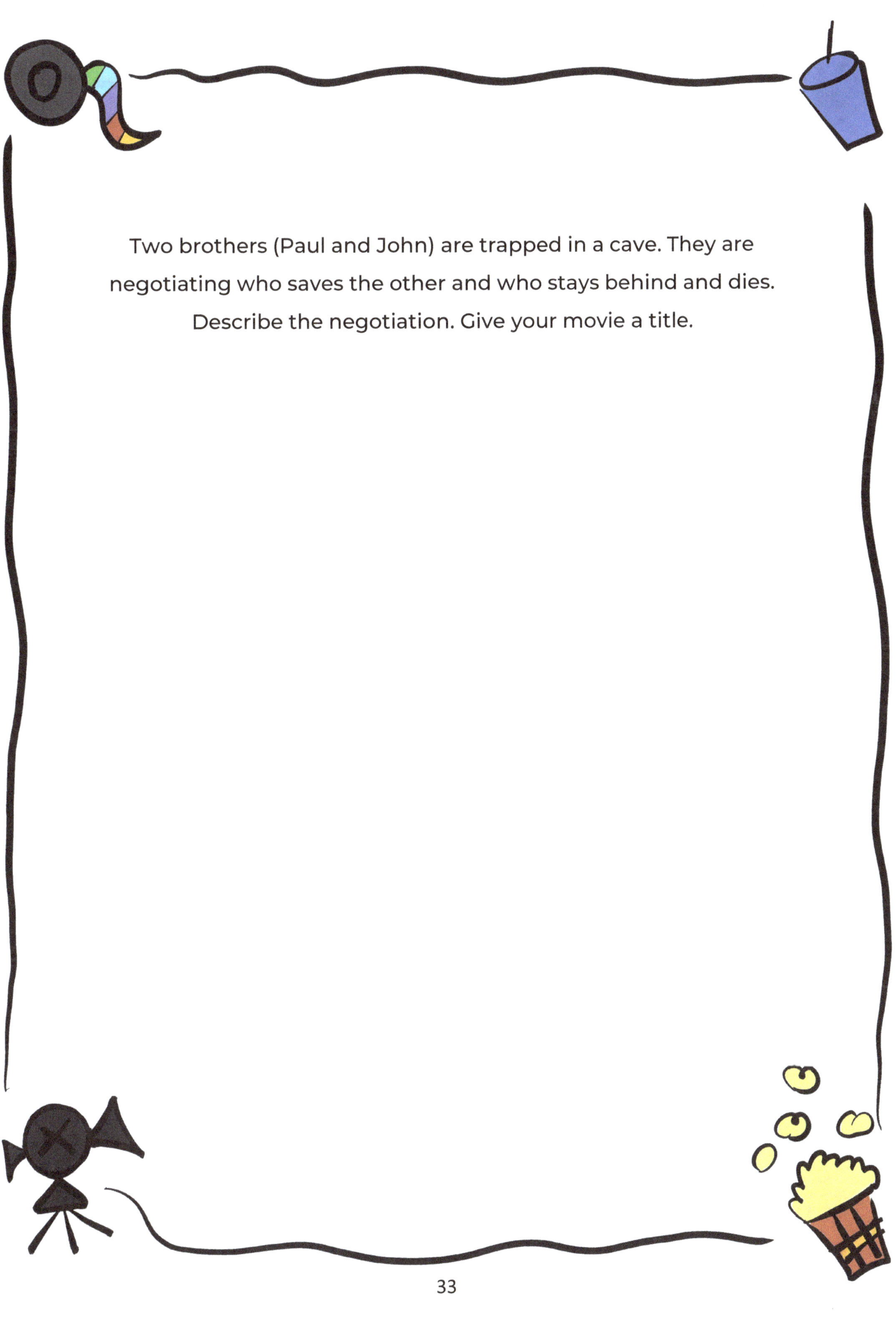

Two brothers (Paul and John) are trapped in a cave. They are negotiating who saves the other and who stays behind and dies. Describe the negotiation. Give your movie a title.

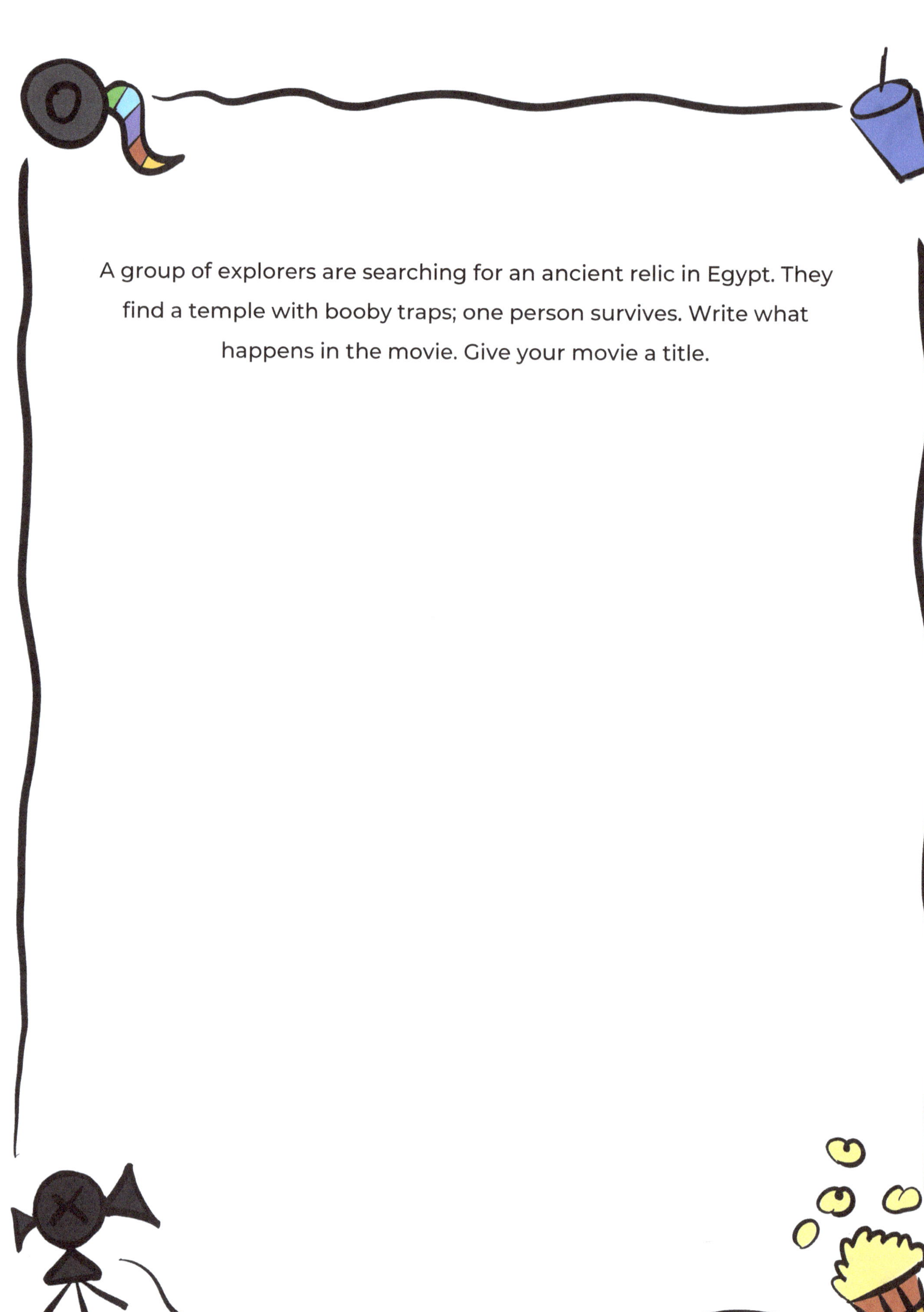

A group of explorers are searching for an ancient relic in Egypt. They find a temple with booby traps; one person survives. Write what happens in the movie. Give your movie a title.

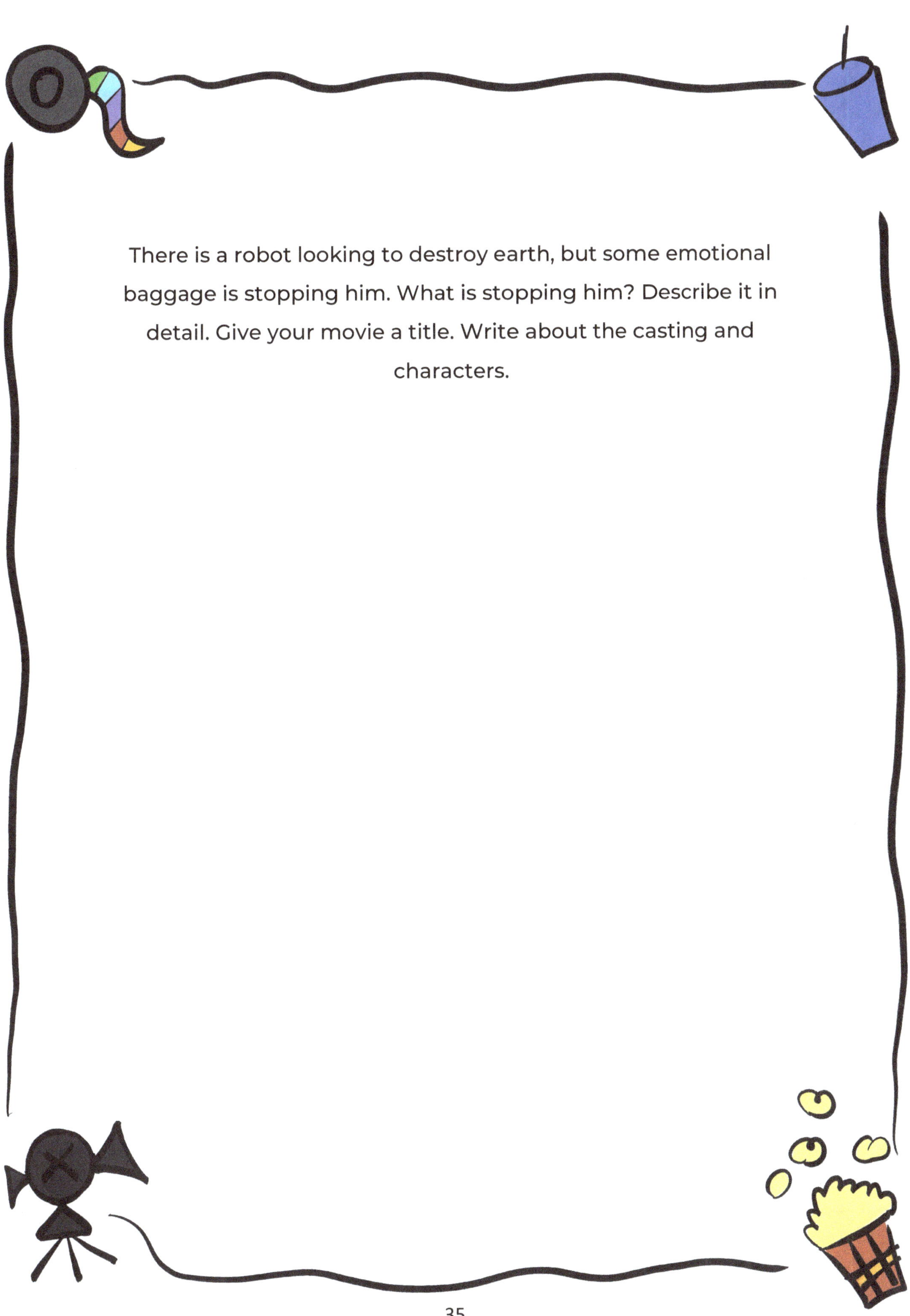

There is a robot looking to destroy earth, but some emotional baggage is stopping him. What is stopping him? Describe it in detail. Give your movie a title. Write about the casting and characters.

In a dark gloomy house, the walls are talking. A frightened mother and child are seated on the bathroom floor. Write what happens in the movie but make it an action flick. Give your movie a title.

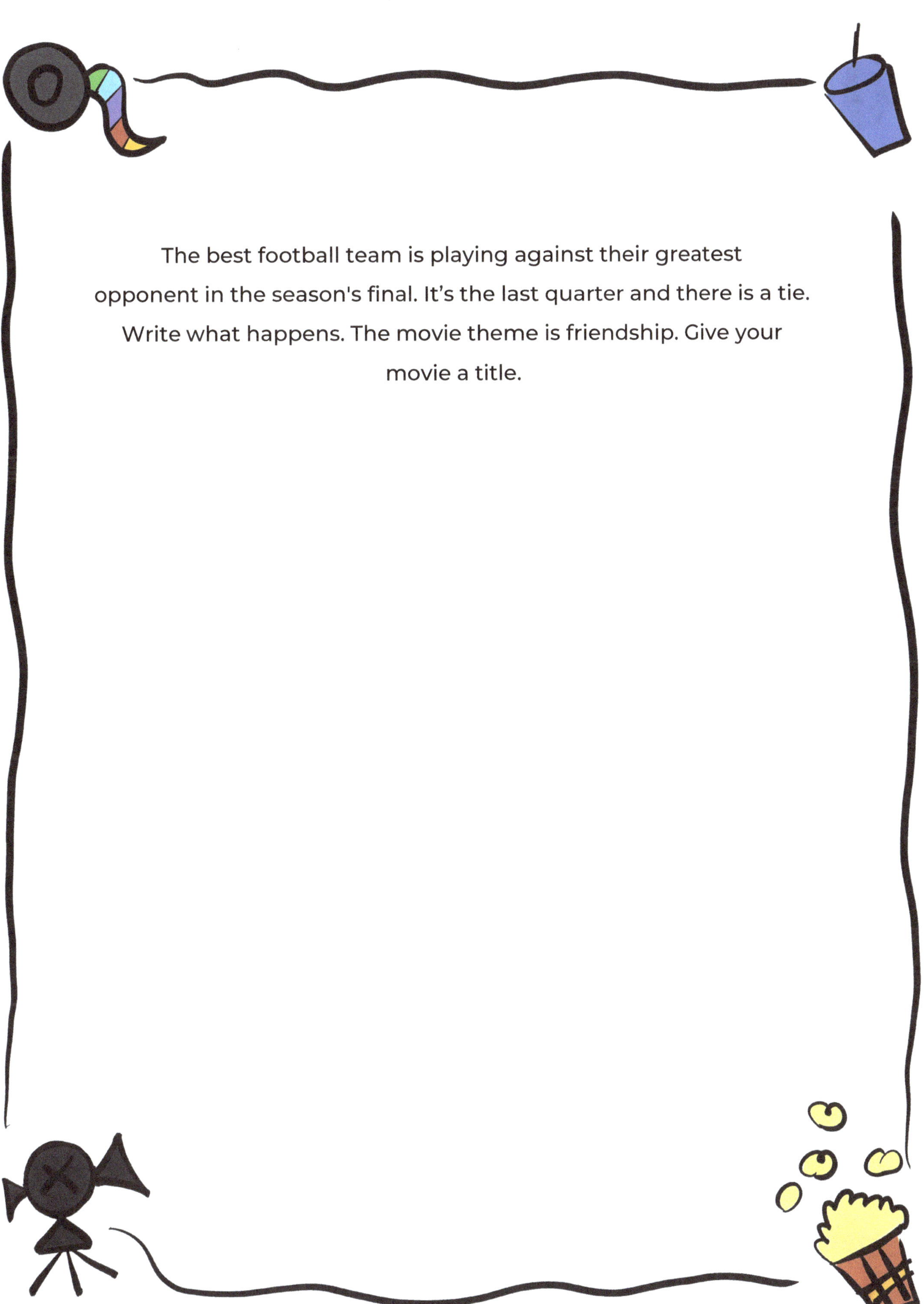

The best football team is playing against their greatest opponent in the season's final. It's the last quarter and there is a tie. Write what happens. The movie theme is friendship. Give your movie a title.

Describe in detail a scene where a robber steals a painting with very fancy high tech. The cop goes to the bathroom every two hours and takes 15 minutes to come back. The painting is inside a tempered glass box that is protected by lasers at all sides of the box. What happens in the movie? Give your movie a title.

– "He will never know". The theme of the movie is lust. Create the movie story. Give your movie a title.

Write a grand finale for an action film in a futuristic war between men and AI machines.

Write a movie story about a loving pet and its owner. Make it a romantic comedy. Give your movie a title. Who would you cast?

Write a funny movie story about a person with any disability who overcomes his or her problems in hilarious ways. Give your movie a title.

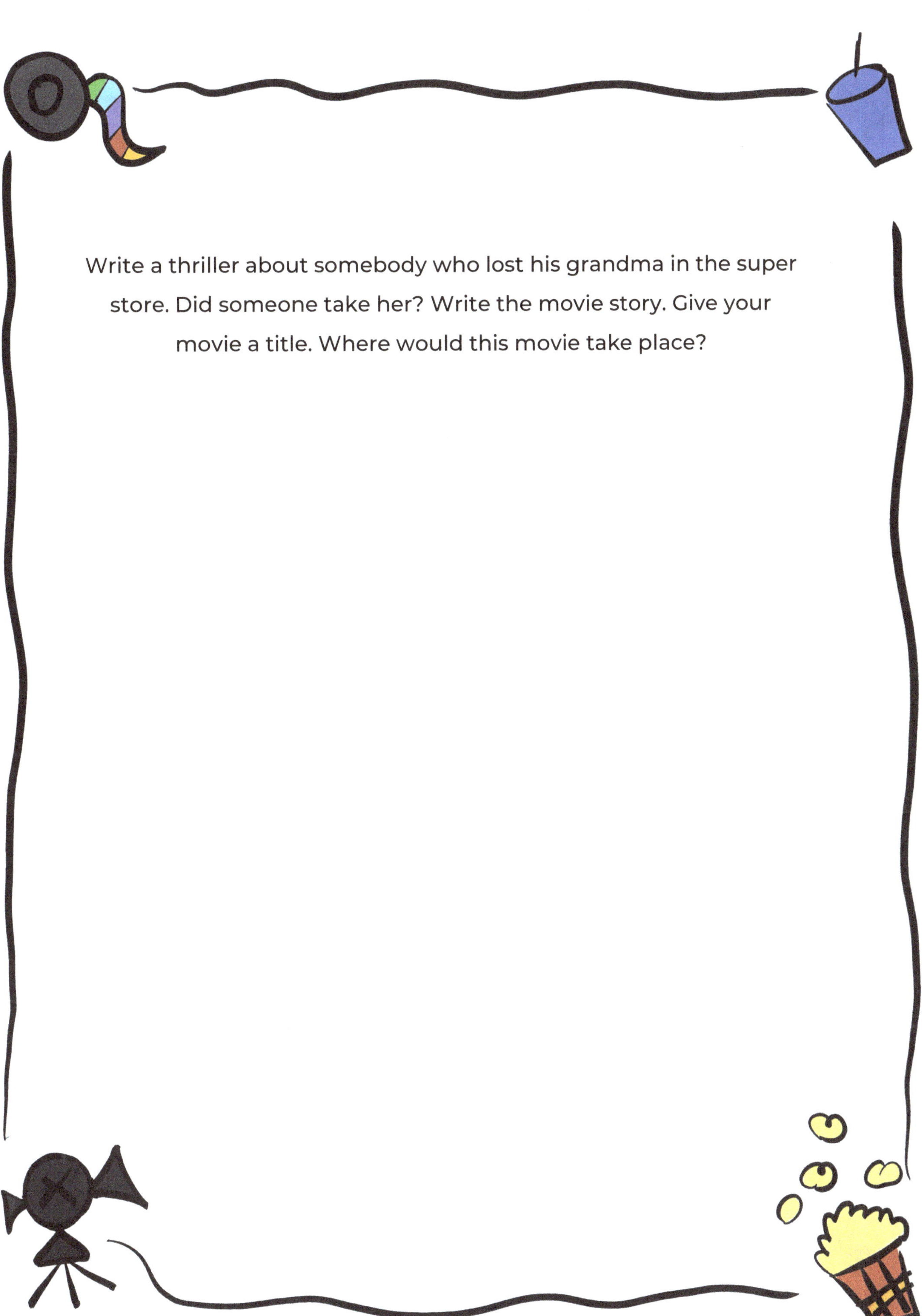

Write a thriller about somebody who lost his grandma in the super store. Did someone take her? Write the movie story. Give your movie a title. Where would this movie take place?

Write a mystery murder movie about five people in a mall. A teacher is murdered. Anyone in the courtyard could have done it. Who did it and why? Write the movie. Give your movie a title.

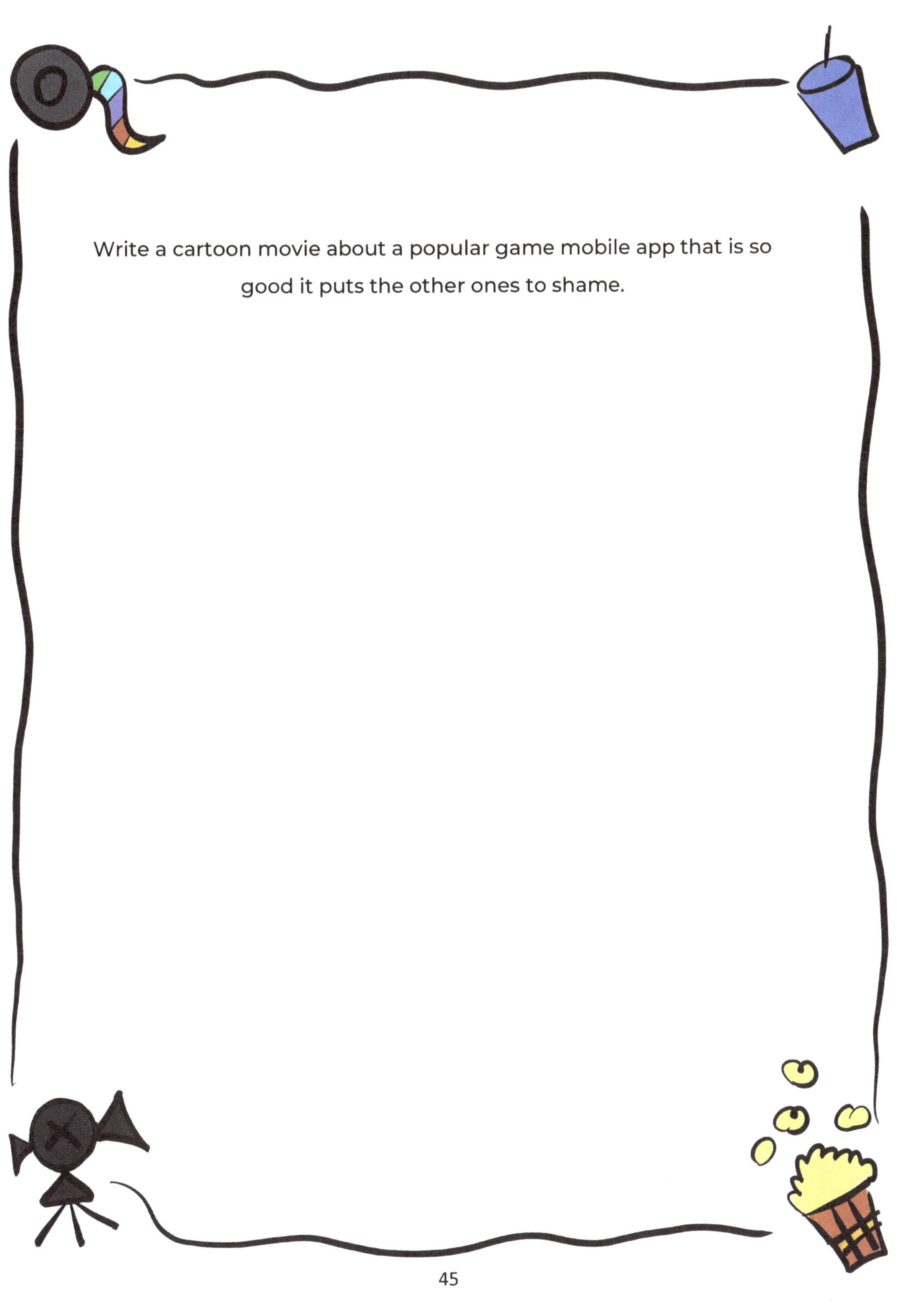

Write a cartoon movie about a popular game mobile app that is so good it puts the other ones to shame.

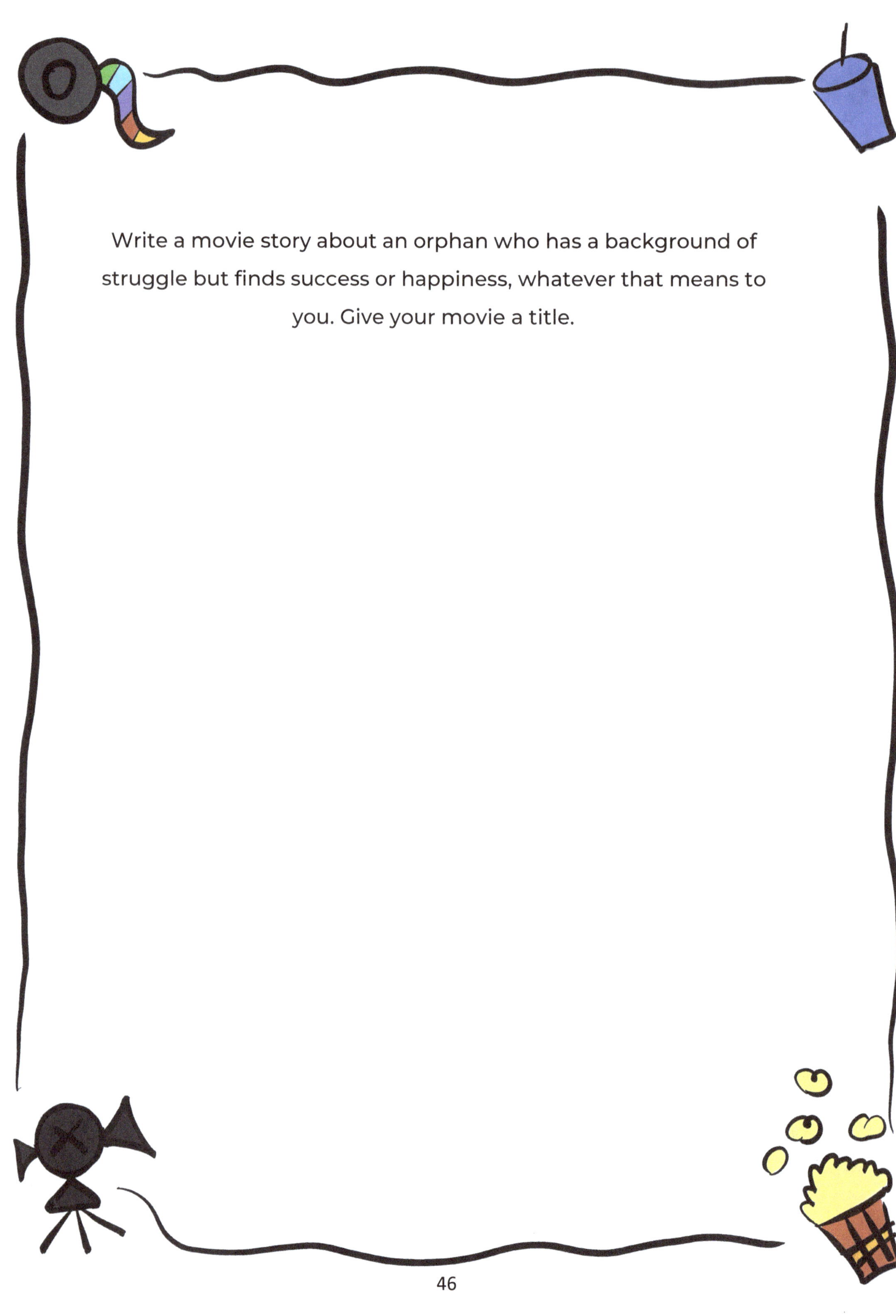

Write a movie story about an orphan who has a background of struggle but finds success or happiness, whatever that means to you. Give your movie a title.

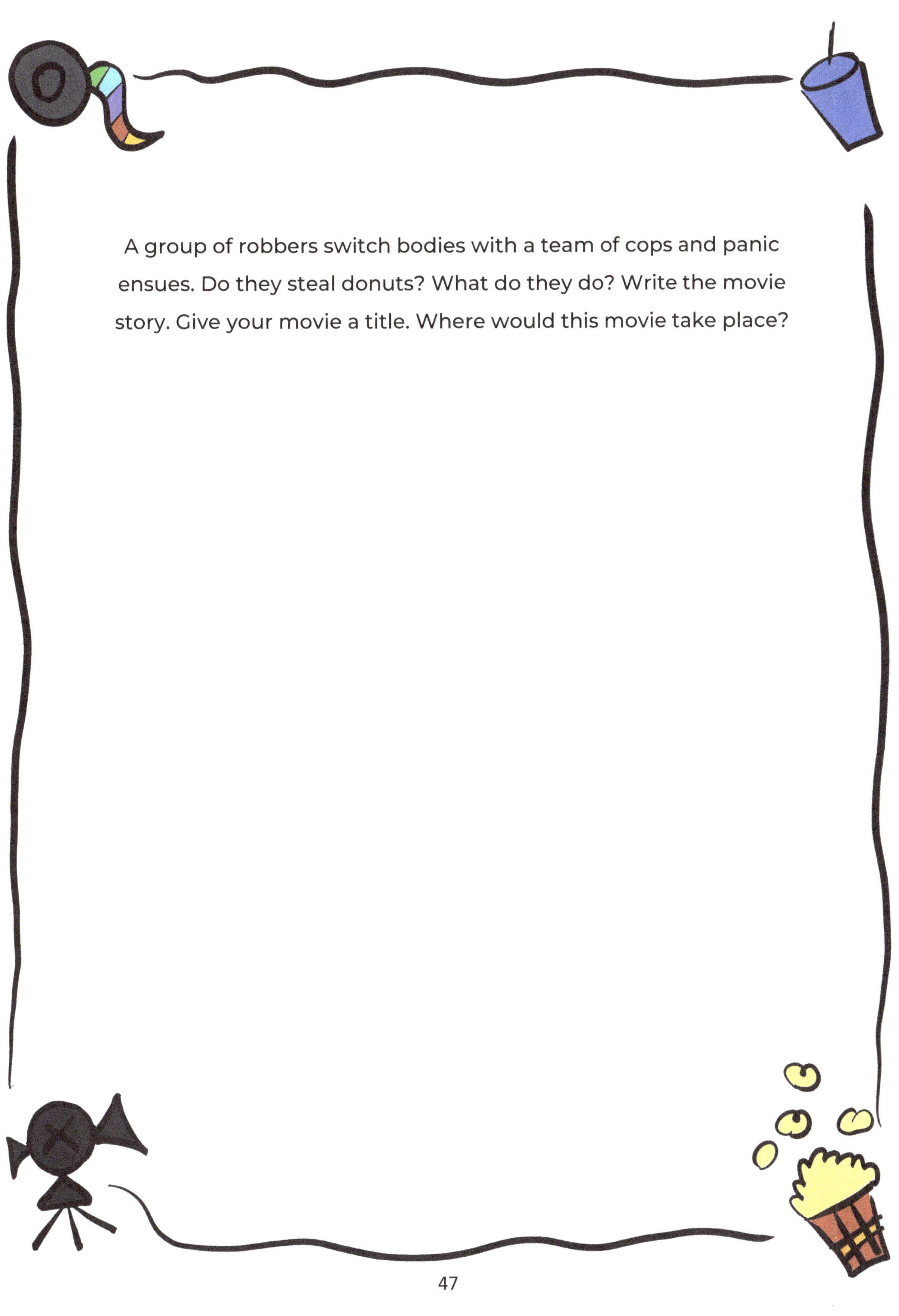

A group of robbers switch bodies with a team of cops and panic ensues. Do they steal donuts? What do they do? Write the movie story. Give your movie a title. Where would this movie take place?

– "Art is dead, don't you understand?" said a character. Write the entire scene. What is the movie about? Write the plot. Give your movie a title.

A family lives in a mansion. It's 1885, the streets are vacant, no one is out there. What is happening? Write the movie story, Give your movie a title. Who would you cast?

A woman wakes up in a hospital and is greeted by a nurse. At first, she feels safe, until a cup of coffee falls on the nurse's lap. She begins to twitch and make weird noises. What happens next? Write the trailer. Give your movie a title.

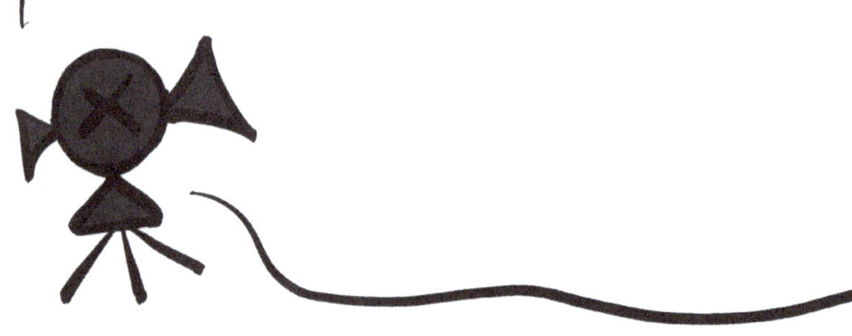

Write a thriller about a retired detective who needs to get back to the force to capture a silent killer. Give your movie a title.

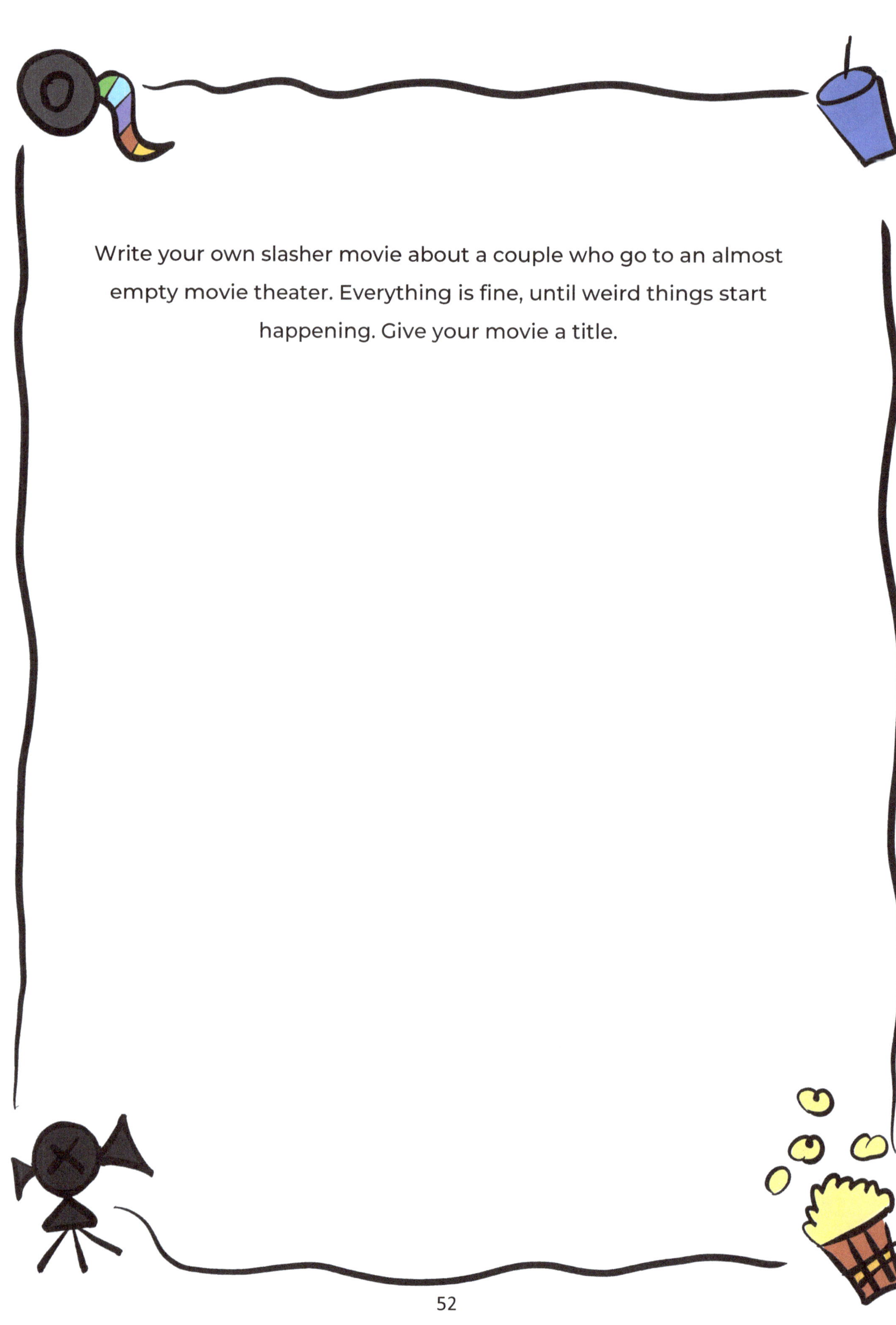

Write your own slasher movie about a couple who go to an almost empty movie theater. Everything is fine, until weird things start happening. Give your movie a title.

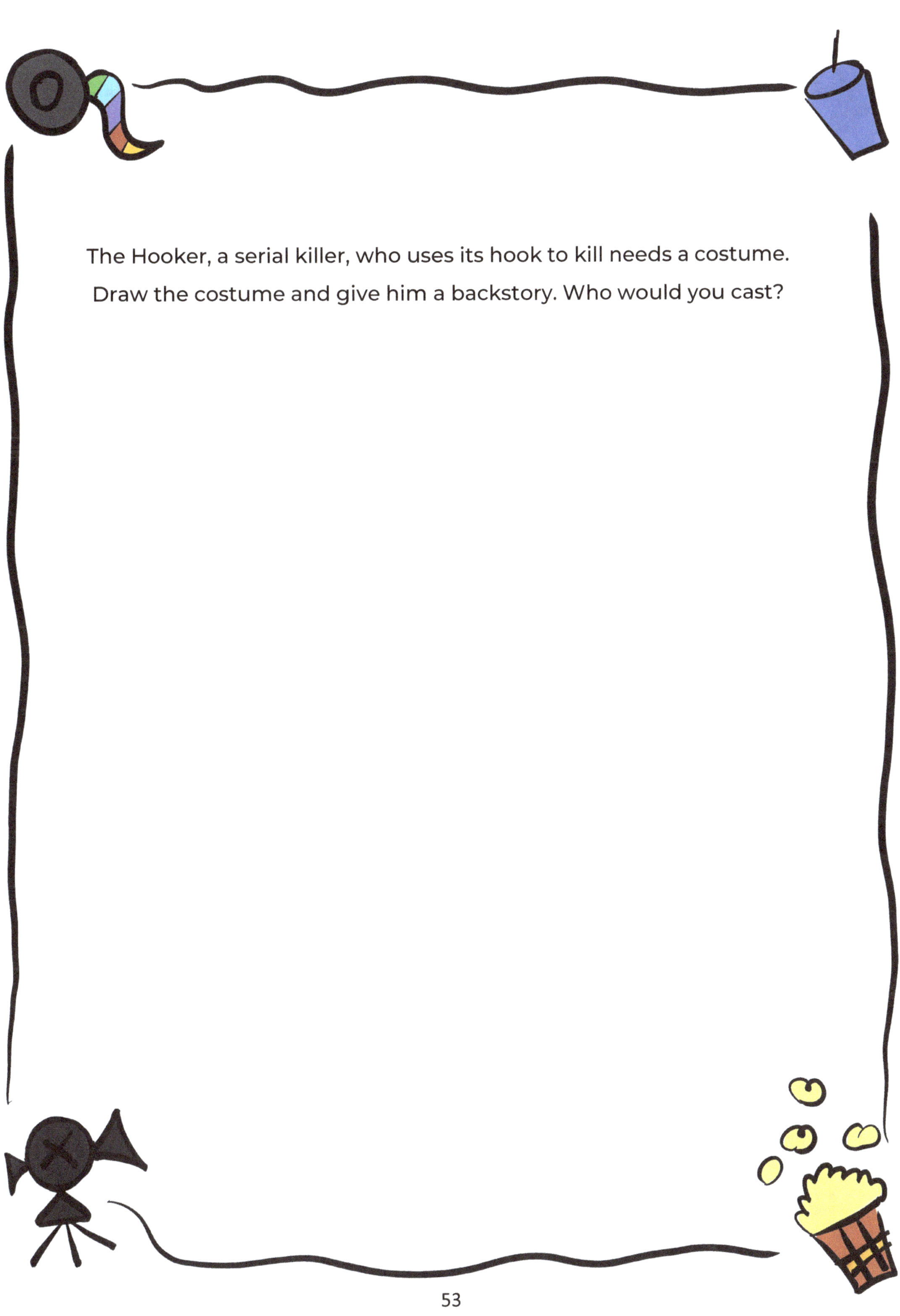

The Hooker, a serial killer, who uses its hook to kill needs a costume. Draw the costume and give him a backstory. Who would you cast?

Create a young adult film about a group of teenagers who need to escape a city. Why do they need to leave? Write the movie story. Give your movie a title. Who would you cast?

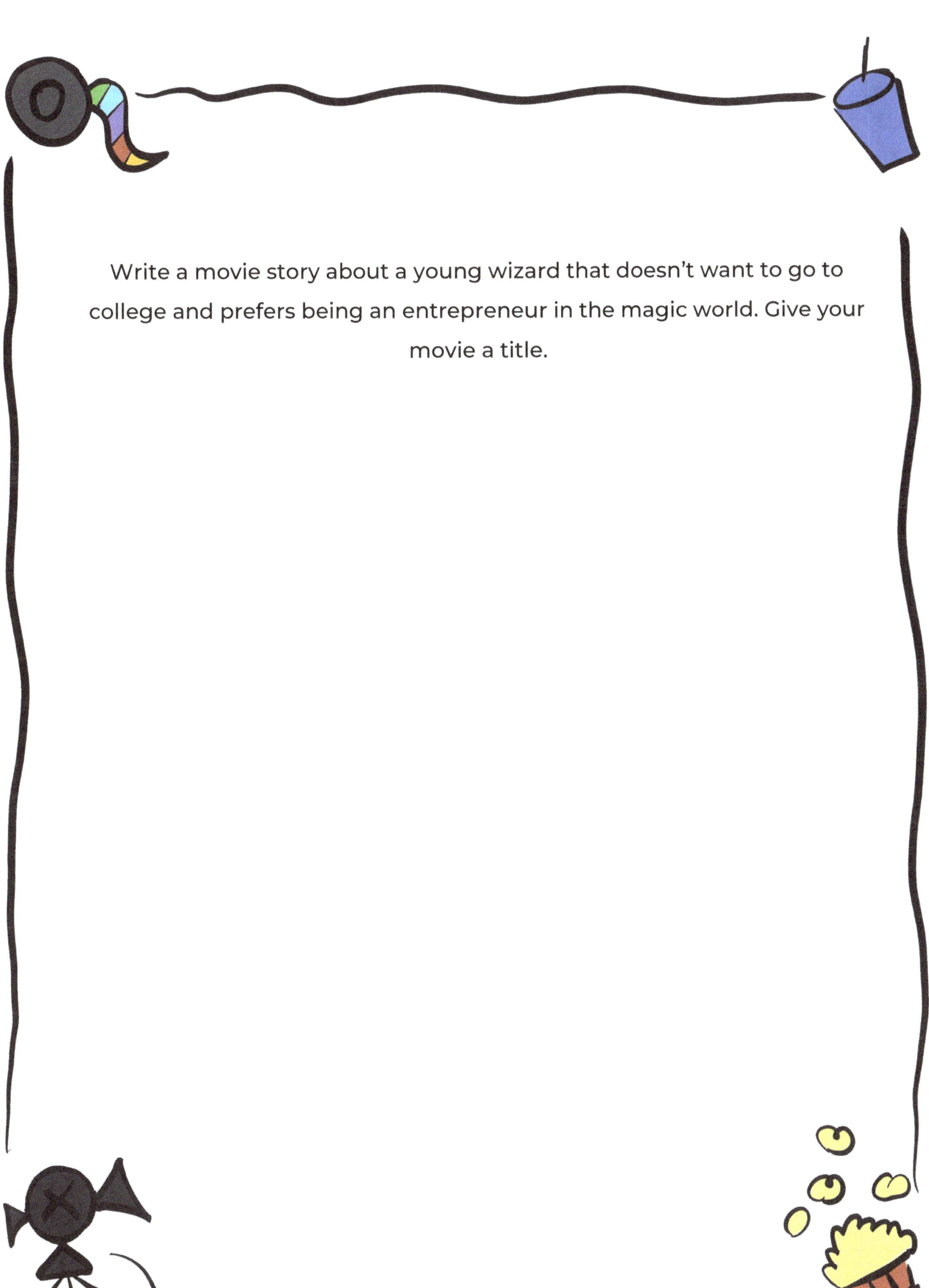

Write a movie story about a young wizard that doesn't want to go to college and prefers being an entrepreneur in the magic world. Give your movie a title.

Create a drama about a woman whose husband is being unfaithful behind her back, she finds out and drains the checking account. What happens next? Write the movie story. Give your movie a title. Who would you cast?

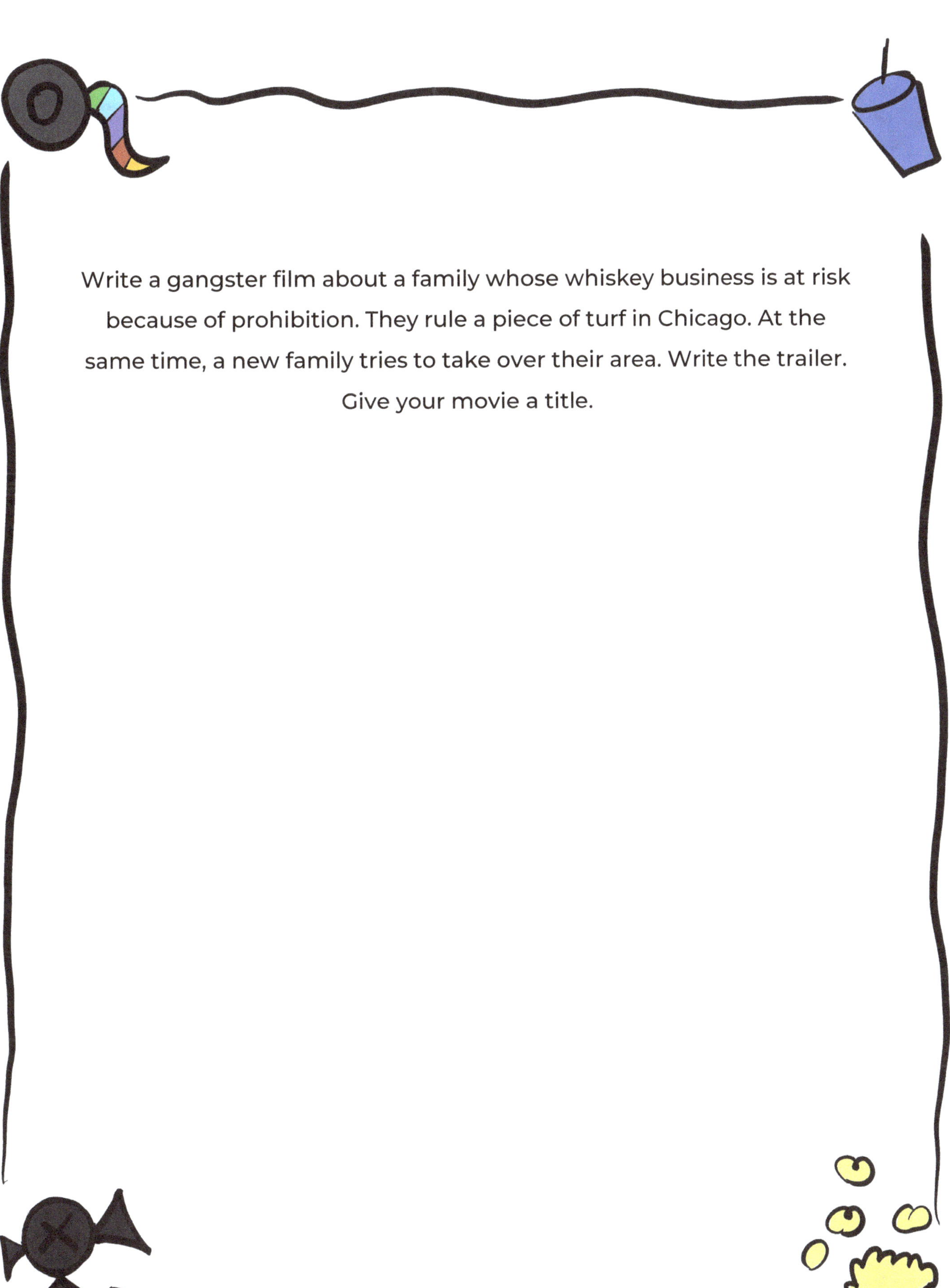

Write a gangster film about a family whose whiskey business is at risk because of prohibition. They rule a piece of turf in Chicago. At the same time, a new family tries to take over their area. Write the trailer. Give your movie a title.

Write a movie story about a young girl imprisoned in a jail on Planet Yaliz 5. All she did was to speak truth to power. Create the movie story and give your movie a title.

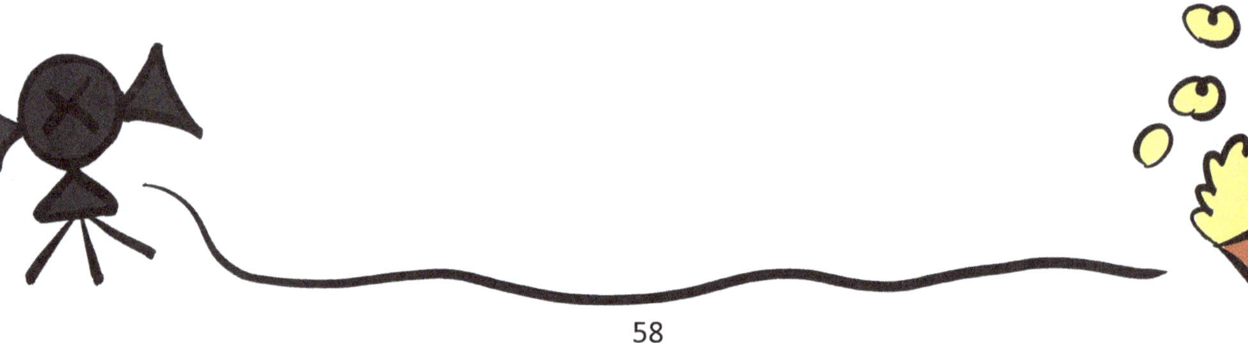

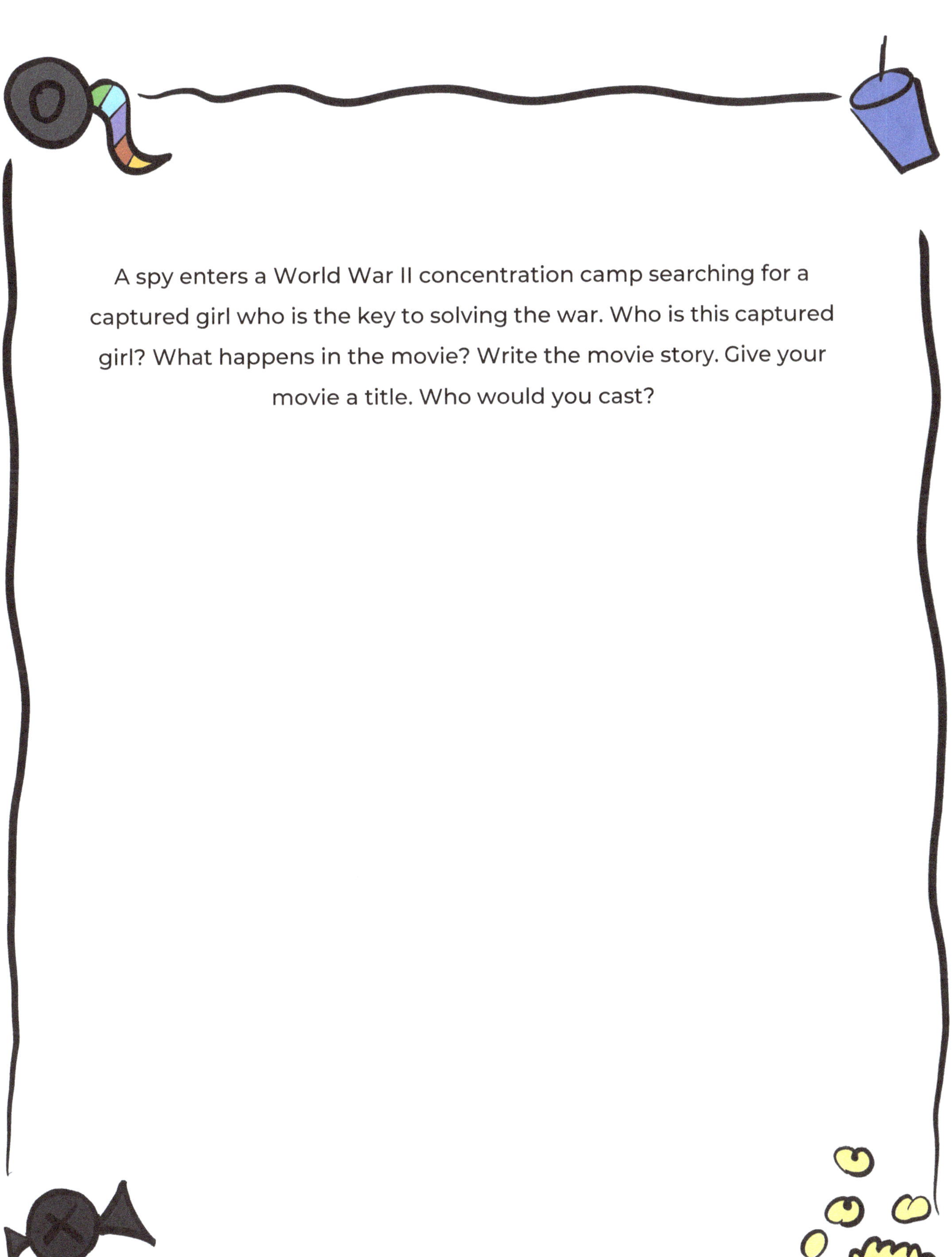

A spy enters a World War II concentration camp searching for a captured girl who is the key to solving the war. Who is this captured girl? What happens in the movie? Write the movie story. Give your movie a title. Who would you cast?

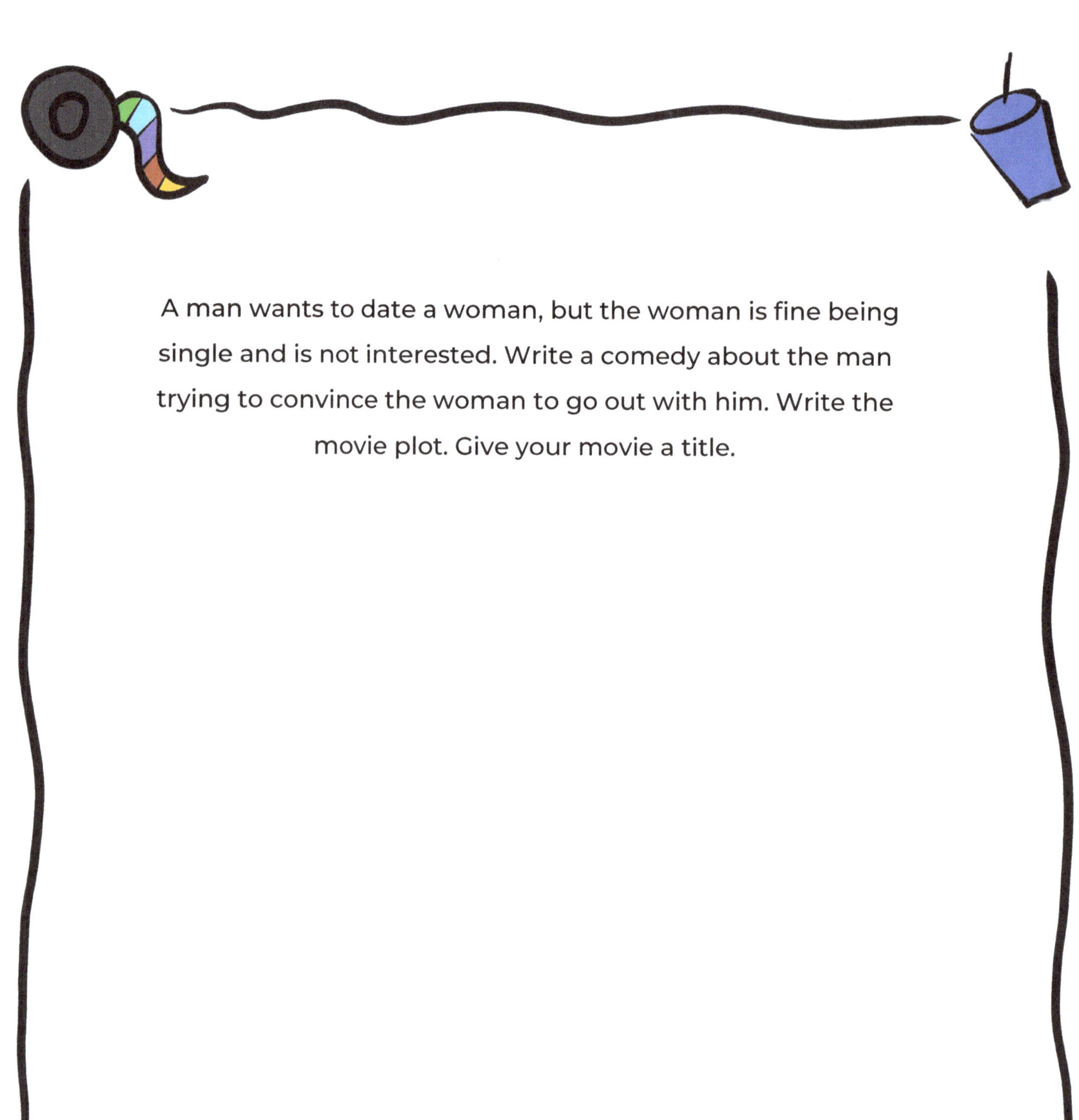

A man wants to date a woman, but the woman is fine being single and is not interested. Write a comedy about the man trying to convince the woman to go out with him. Write the movie plot. Give your movie a title.

Now write the other way around; a woman is trying to get a man to date her. The man is not interested. Make it a drama. Give your movie a title.

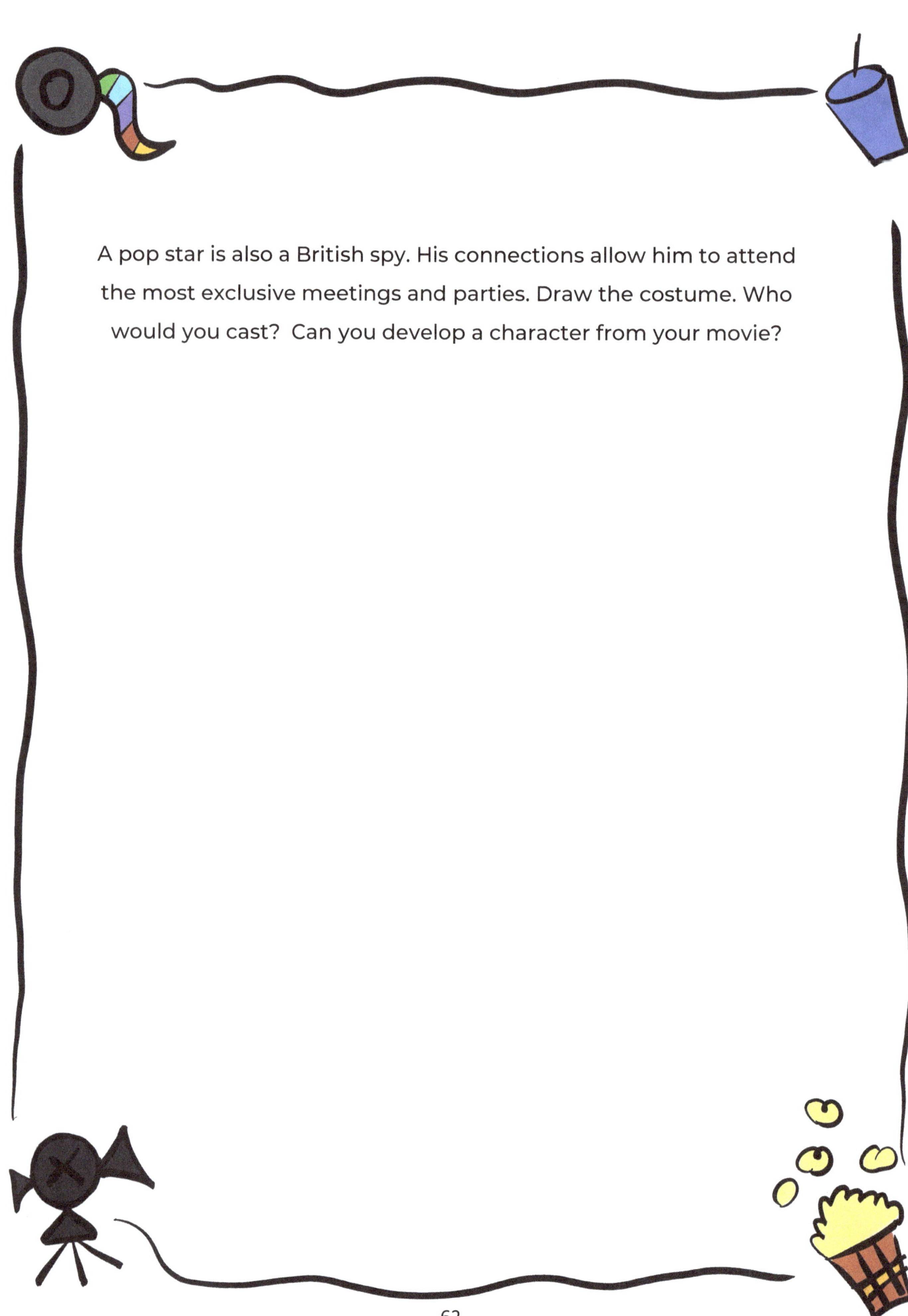

A pop star is also a British spy. His connections allow him to attend the most exclusive meetings and parties. Draw the costume. Who would you cast? Can you develop a character from your movie?

Create a movie plot about a cartoon animal, who is left on the street by her owner. Describe her journey towards a new home. Give your movie a title. Who would voice the characters?

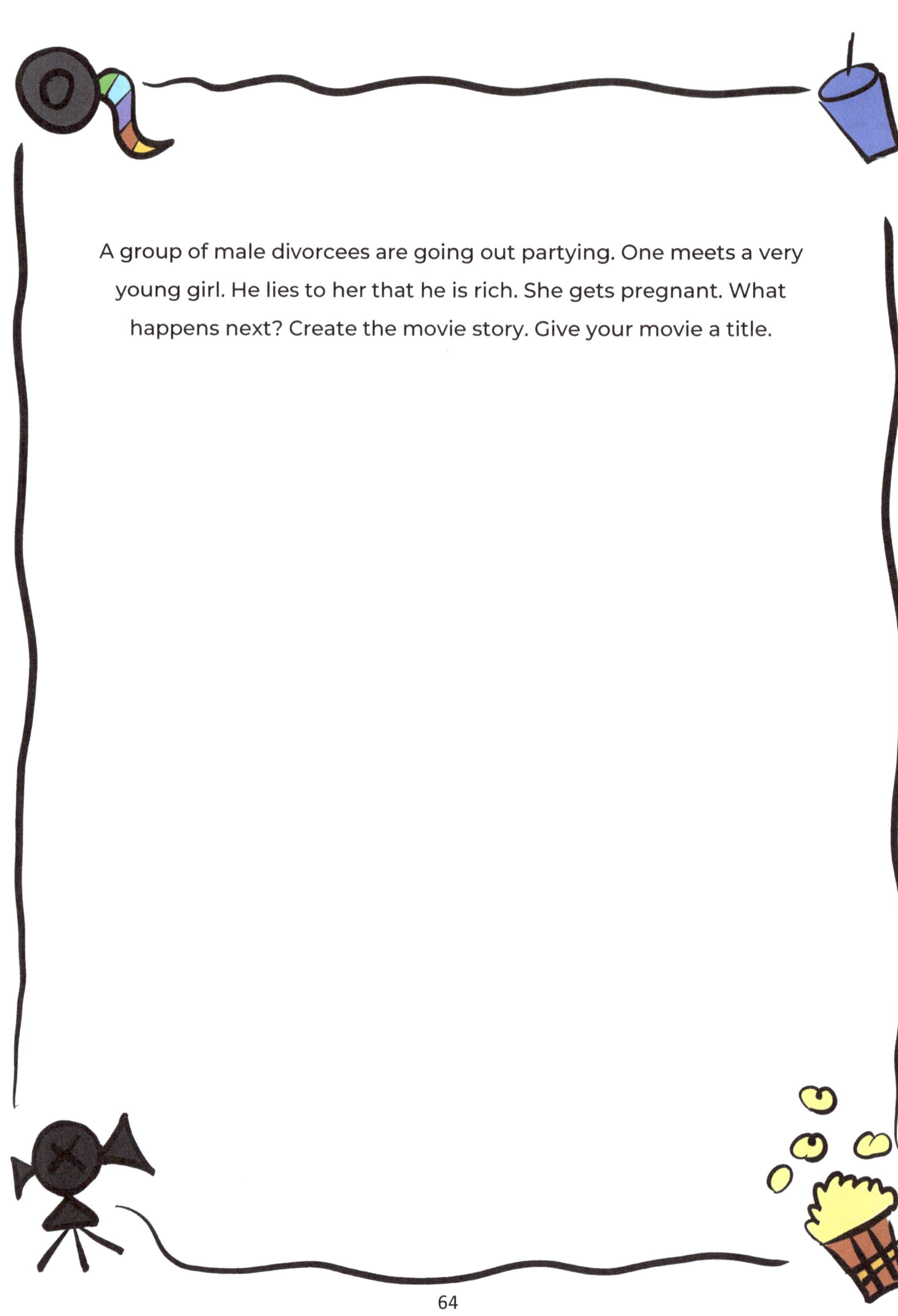

A group of male divorcees are going out partying. One meets a very young girl. He lies to her that he is rich. She gets pregnant. What happens next? Create the movie story. Give your movie a title.

Draw a scene from the movie in page 62

Draw a scene from the movie in page 61

Draw a scene from the movie in page 39.

Draw a scene from the movie in page 29.

Draw a scene from the movie in page 10.

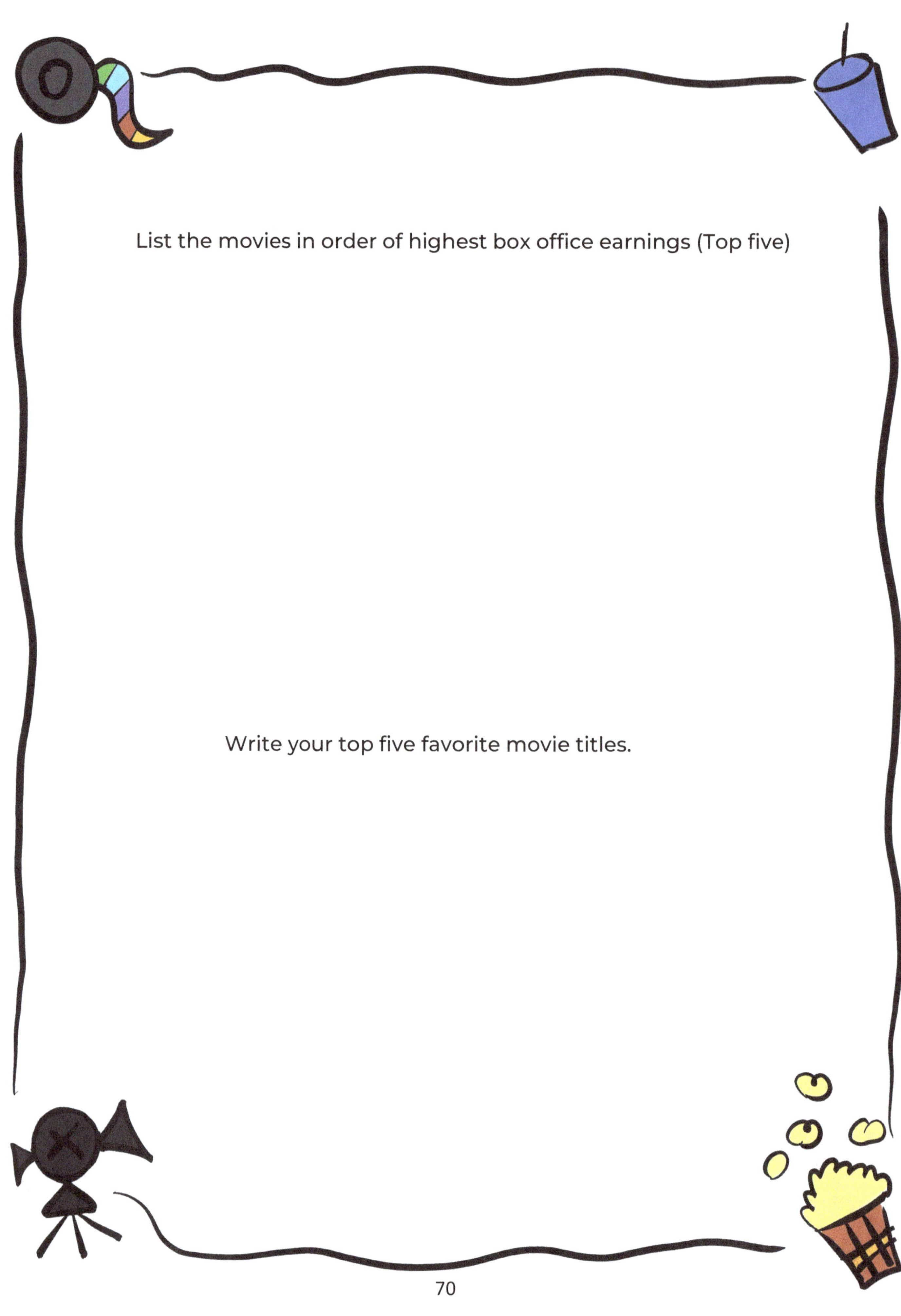

List the movies in order of highest box office earnings (Top five)

Write your top five favorite movie titles.

 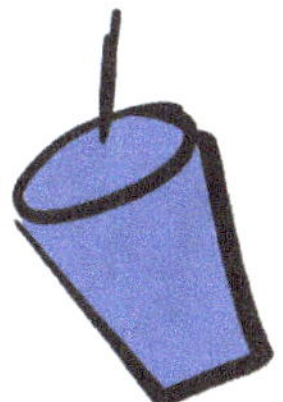

Write your top five favorite movies you created.

Movie Awards

Best Picture:_________________________________

Best Character Male:_____________________________

Best Character Female:____________________________

Best Supportive Character: _____________________

Thank you for buying this book!

I hope you like it.

If you wish, you can follow me on this link: